Carmel Bird grew up in Tasmania and now lives in Castlemaine, Victoria. She has published two other books on writing: *Writing the Story of Your Life* and *Not Now Jack – I'm Writing a Novel*. As well as publishing many novels and collections of short fiction, she has edited several anthologies including *The Penguin Century of Australian Stories* and *The Stolen Children – Their Stories*.
www.carmelbird.com

Remembering

McPhee Gribble

PRAISE FOR CARMEL BIRD

'Carmel Bird is a gifted writer and an exemplary teacher of writing. As someone who has carefully and thoughtfully analysed her own craft, Carmel is able to forensically diagnose the strengths and weaknesses of a piece of writing. Coupled with Carmel's generous and creative ability to empathise with the author's ambitions, her advice will help many realise their potential.'
JULIANNE SCHULTZ, *Griffith Review*

Automatic Teller

'Carmel Bird writes fiction every bit as spectacular as Angela Carter's.'
MICHAEL SHARKEY

'Carmel Bird uses structure and syntax the way a witch uses spells.'
CLEO Magazine

'Carmel Bird's enthusiasm is so engaging, and this book such a wonderful catalogue of creative cause and effect, that for every wanna-be writer it sends into the forest to bring down trees in search of manuscripts, I have little doubt it will send three or four readers into bookshops or libraries in search of books.'
IAN MCFARLANE, *Canberra Times*

The Woodpecker Toy Fact

'*The Woodpecker Toy Fact* is my sort of book.'
GERALD MURNANE

The Bluebird Café

'A writer who is willing to take risks, breaking away from the routine and the fashionable.'
ANDREW REIMER

Cherry Ripe

'Demonic, savage and funny.'
DAVID MYERS

The Common Rat
'A deadpan Tasmanian directness which can charm and startle.'
DENNIS DAVISON

Child of the Twilight
'Fresh and brilliant. The sort of book that keeps on unfolding in the imagination long after you've finished reading it.'
GABRIELLE LORD

Red Shoes
'There is something of Vonnegut or Mark Twain in her deadpan, mock ironies.'
PETER GOLDSWORTHY

The White Garden
'A clever, wise and humane triumph.'
The Australian

The Essential Bird
'Bird's prose shines with spilt laughter and celebratory irony.'
The Age

'... deep-dyed rhetoric, gorgeous and perfumed.'
The Sunday Age

'Bird's prose delights in coincidences and conundrums, in the playful dangerous blend of fact and fiction.'
Canberra Times

Writing the Story of Your Life
'This book, so inspiring, generous and thorough, will show you the real joy of writing a memoir.'
MARION HALLIGAN

Dear Writer
'*Dear Writer* – I love it.'
MEM FOX

SPINELESS WONDERS
ABN98156041888
PO Box 220 STRAWBERRY HILLS
New South Wales, Australia, 2012
www.shortaustralianstories.com.au

Dear Writer Revisited first published by Spineless Wonders 2013
Dear Writer first published by McPhee Gribble in 1988 and republished by Random House Australia in 1996

Text copyright © Carmel Bird
Cover design by Girrahween Designs
Layout by Bronwyn Mehan

'Woodpecker image' by Paul Singer from The Concise Encyclopaedia of Birds
by Bertel Brun, Illustrations by Paul Singer
Published by Octopus Books 59 Grosvenor Street, London 1974

All rights reserved. Without limiting the rights under copyright reserved above, no part of this publication may be produced, stored in or introduced into a retrieval sysem, or transmitted, in any form or by any means (electronic, mechanical, photocopying, recording or otherwise), without the prior written permission of the publisher of this book.

Typeset in Adobe Garamond Pro
Printed and bound by Lightning Source Australia

National Library of Australia Cataloguing-in-Publication entry
Dear Writer Revisited/Carmel Bird
1st ed.
978-0-9874479-6-8 (pbk.)
808.3

Dear Writer Revisited
The Classic Guide to Writing Fiction

Carmel Bird

Contents

xvi
Foreword
Introduction
Author's Introduction to the 2013 Edition

1
Letter One
So You Want to be Agatha Christie
The Importance of Writing About
Things You Know

8
Letter Two
'A' for Alive, 'D' for Dead
The Use of Adverbs and Adjectives

14
Letter Three
Top and Tail
Looking at Beginnings and Endings

20
Letter Four
The Omniscient Author
Choice of Point of View

27
Letter Five
Giving Up Housework
DEDICATION TO THE WRITER'S TASK

31
Letter Six
The Name of Your Angel is Desire
ABOUT WRITER'S BLOCK

37
Letter Seven
The Centre of the Mystery
FURTHER THOUGHTS ON THE IMPORTANCE OF PERSONAL EXPERIENCE

43
Letter Eight
Stranger than Fiction
MAKING THE READER BELIEVE THINGS

49
Letter Nine
The Thought Experiment
THE ROLE OF THE IMAGINATION IN THE CREATION OF FICTION

56
Letter Ten
Baby's Name
FINDING A TITLE FOR YOUR STORY

64
Letter Eleven
Cause of Death
SOME POINTS TO CHECK WHEN REVISING STORIES

72
Letter Twelve
In the Beginning was the Quill
A DISCUSSION OF PENS, TYPEWRITERS AND WORD PROCESSORS

77
Letter Thirteen
Dear Diary
KEEPING JOURNALS, NOTEBOOKS, SCRAPBOOKS

82
Letter Fourteen
Practical Matters
BECOMING FAMILIAR WITH THE EVERYDAY WORLD OF WRITING

85
Letter Fifteen
Writers Are Different
A WAY OF LIFE

90
Letter Sixteen
Pepper And Salt
OVERSTATEMENT AND UNDERSTATEMENT

95
Letter Seventeen
Getting into Print
WHEN YOUR WORK IS PUBLISHED

100
Letter Eighteen
The Manuscript
PREPARATION AND SUBMISSION

104
Letter Nineteen
Sources of Inspiration
WHERE IDEAS COME FROM

110
Letter Twenty
The Ear and the Heart
THE RHYTHMS OF PROSE

114
Letter Twenty-One
When All's Said and Done
THE FINAL DRAFT

117
Story One and Analysis
'The Company of Laughing Singing Invisibles'

132
Story Two and Analysis
The Writing Mechanism and Writing to Order
'From Paradise To Wonderland'

146
Afterword

147
Acknowledgements

150
Index

Foreword

INTRODUCTION

Author's Introduction to the 2013 Edition

Dear Writer Revisited is a collection of letters from an experienced writer to a woman who has sent her own stories to be assessed. The book was first published, as *Dear Writer*, in 1988, when people used typewriters and primitive computers, and posted manuscripts off in envelopes. Although the way things are done has changed, the principles of writing fiction have not, as readers of the letters will realise.

I am writing this preface in 2013. So many things about the world of writing, publishing, reading have changed in dramatic ways, and are still changing. A couple of years ago *Dear Writer* went out of print, yet I still get emails from universities and individuals asking for multiple copies which I can no longer supply. I have spent a long time now considering how best to deliver the old-fashioned truths expressed in *Dear Writer* into the minds of writers in 2013 plus. I finally decided that I would construct an eBook and would present the letters to 'Dear Writer' in an almost unedited form, including the anachronisms embodied in the quaint notion of 'letters'. So the body of this new edition is more or

INTRODUCTION

less the old *Dear Writer*, but I figured I would need to discuss at the beginning some of the sharp differences between what it was to be a writer in 1988, and what it is to be a writer in 2013. The reader who hopes to be a writer can read the central *Dear Writer* letters as a kind of historical narrative that contains lessons on the essence of the writer's art, while being aware that the book acknowledges the new and ever-evolving world of writing. I realised that if I started discussing the role of blogs and tweets and so forth the material could be out of date before sunset. Today, Virginia and Writer would, at the very least, be exchanging emails, and the history of their correspondence could be collected in an email archive and even published in hard copy and/or eBook. I have heard of one (no doubt there are others) book of collected literary emails, *Distant Intimacy: A friendship in the age of the internet* by Frederic Raphael and Joseph Epstein. But all I am saying is that the world of letter writer Virginia O'Day and the nameless woman known as 'Dear Writer' is closer to the *world* of Charles Dickens and Jane Austen than it is to the world of a budding writer today. Yet I believe it is also true to say that the principles presented in the letters hold good for a writer in the nineteenth, twentieth and twenty-first centuries.

INTRODUCTION TO THE 1996 EDITION

As a writer of fiction and as a teacher of fiction writing, I know that the techniques of writing can be taught. This statement is sometimes challenged by people who believe that the techniques of fiction writing cannot be taught. I find the arguments of these doubters curious; our education system is based on the idea (which appears to go undisputed) that children will be taught to read and write and so on, and it seems evident to me that people can be taught to play the flute, to swim, to perform brain surgery – to do anything you can think of. Why would writing fiction be different? Nobody suggests that all flautists will display the talents of James Galway, and I do not suggest that a teacher can give a student of writing the talent to write, yet I know that students can be taught many of the techniques they will need, that talent can be discovered, nurtured, developed.

However, writing fiction involves more than the mastering of technique. A writer needs to be a reader, to know how to read, and how to think about reading and writing. Needs to understand something about the history of fiction and to know a great deal about the present context, the present world of writing. It seems to me that a writer needs to be aware of what else is being written these days, of how other writers' work is being received by readers.

It can sometimes help to belong to writers' organisations, to subscribe to newsletters that tell you about opportunities for the publication of your work, or of workshops you can go to, seminars, festivals. At festivals, for instance, you can meet and listen to experienced writers talking about all aspects of writing and being a writer; you can meet publishers and editors and agents and so on. Students of writing do well to read the books pages of the newspapers, and to subscribe to some literary magazines. It always surprises me how few students who go to classes in writing have an understanding of these things. Something that they certainly do learn from classes is the way they can connect with the context of writing, with, if you like, the world of, the culture of, the writer.

Actually, what with the technology, the paper, the ink, the subscriptions to magazines, the buying of books, the postage, faxes and phone calls, the photocopying, the attendances at

INTRODUCTION

festivals and all the rest of it, being a writer requires quite a financial investment on your part, as well as the investment of your time, your emotions, your heart, not to mention your soul. But more of all that later. Subscribing to all the magazines in the world, and going to all the writers' festivals, will not improve your writing, but can give you vital information about the so-called world of writing. You need to know this stuff.

If you decide to enrol in a course in writing, and are searching for the right one, I suggest you seek out a tutor whose own writing you admire in some way. There are at least two parts to a writing teacher – the writing and the teaching. Can he write? Can he teach? It's too late to find this out after you have given your money and your time. And I think it is worth pointing out that writing classes are not mandatory; you can easily write fiction without ever having taken a class – or been to a festival or watched a writer speaking on television. When it comes down to it, the principal thing a writer has to do is write, to sit down at the desk and make up stories. You can actually guess and glean for yourself all the info about the so-called world of writing; you can work out how to present a manuscript to a publisher, if you want to. You can pick up some ideas from books such as this one. In classes and at festivals I have sometimes felt that students and members of the audience were hoping to be given the secret to a magic formula that was supposed to be in the possession of the tutor or speaker. The secret is that there is no magic formula.

Writing students have sometimes told me they wish for a book that will not only provide advice about skills, but will somehow urge and inspire the reader to write and continue to write. I hope that *Dear Writer* will fulfil the students' wishes and answer the needs of both new and experienced writers.

I believe that fiction writers find the material for fiction in their own memories of life – it's what their imaginations do with that material that characterises the fiction. Books, films, newspapers, television and so on give people a lot of information which acts as a sort of secondhand memory. This kind of material can be a source of inspiration, but when much of the content of the fiction is borrowed from this source, without passing through the particular medium of the writer's heart and imagination, the fiction can fail to engage the reader, can be dull and unconvincing. This is not a blunt exhortation to write in a simple-minded way about the facts you know while ignoring the possibilities of the things you don't know; rather I am suggesting that one of the finest and purest and most exciting and inventive and rewarding elements of the writing of fiction is the imagination of the writer. But the first field of the writer's enquiry actually *is* the writer. Find out who you are and what you know, and then more or less forget it – fly off wide of your own base.

'The heart knows things, and so does the imagination. Thank God. If not for the heart and imagination, the world of fiction would be a pretty seedy place. It might not even exist at all.'
STEPHEN KING

'The fiction arose out of the unconscious, coupled with observation but above all with imagination.'
DAPHNE DU MAURIER

INTRODUCTION

Recently I was talking to a man who had been kind enough to send me a lot of research material for one of my books. During the conversation the man asked me how I was going to use the material. His question prompted me to come up with a useful and straightforward explanation – I said that I would read all the papers he had sent me, I would take some notes, then I would more or less forget the material and make stuff up.

That would be the novel.

> *'He who cannot howl will not find his pack.'*
> CHARLES SIMIC

The more you write, the more you explore, the more you will surprise yourself with who you are and what you can think. There are moments of inspiration and vision and illumination which come, it seems unbidden, and it is the joyous task of the artist, the writer, to recognise these moments and to respond to them. And this is not to suggest that writers must wait upon inspiration – quite the opposite. You get to the desk and you write anyway, come what may, and if visions and illuminations come, rejoice. And keep writing.

I emphasise my belief, based on my own experience as a writer, and strengthened by my observation of the progress of many students, that the first, the original and primary source for the material of fiction is in the life, the experience, the memory, the self of the writer. When the writer is truly drawing on the source of the self, the techniques of writing fiction seem to come naturally, requiring little discussion, presenting few problems. The earliest writing may well be largely autobiographical, but this will soon move on as you become more familiar with yourself as a writer. That might sound like a funny thing to say – after all, you are you, how can there be any difference between you as you and you as writer? I reckon there is a difference, and it is largely this difference that causes problems for friends and families when people start up, apparently out of the blue, as writers. I talk about this in Letter Five, and also in *Not Now Jack – I'm Writing a Novel*. Suddenly you are someone who is seeing the world in a new way; suddenly your friends are perhaps part of your material and they might get jumpy about that.

I have seen that the process of all this can be painful in a number of ways. Looking into yourself is the most difficult and demanding part; then there is the new relationship you have to develop with the people around you, and with, I think, all of life. You are in the process of evolution. I set out to guide students by nurture, by stealth and by shock. The reader of the letters to *Dear Writer* can expect the same treatment.

People who are beginning to write fiction, particularly people living in remote places, often send their manuscripts to an assessor, and the letters in *Dear Writer* were inspired by correspondence I had with writers when I was reading their manuscripts. A reader probably should be an anonymous person, and so I used to sign my letters with the name of a character from my own fiction. Her name is Virginia O'Day, and she has signed the letters to 'Dear Writer'. (The novel in which Virginia appears is *The Bluebird Café* which was in fact published *after* the first publication of *Dear Writer*. When Virginia was appearing in public as the author of the letters, she was also being created as a teenage anorexic in the novel. It now feels strange and interesting to go back and revise her letters.)

INTRODUCTION

'It is play, not properness, that is the central artery, the core, the brainstem of creative life.'
CLARISSA PINKOLA ESTÉS

In these letters I have said the process of becoming a writer can be painful. Sometimes I think that the writer's voice, for want of a better term, can never be found without pain. It is much, much easier not to write fiction, you know. Writing fiction is something you decide to do all by yourself; it also is something you actually do all by yourself (and it can be very lonely indeed). You may well discover things about yourself (in the process of writing) that you would prefer not to have known. The exploration of the self in the course of writing is sometimes compared with the process of psychoanalysis. I think there are probably similarities, but I see a significant difference: at the end of analysis (supposing analysis ever ends) the patient, better or worse, or at least, changed in some way, is the product. After the self-examinations involved in the writing of fiction, the writer will have some stories that have been written down for other people to read. You have a product, a work, perhaps, of art, something to share, something with which to go public. *Stop, look, listen!* you are saying to the world.

And if they are going to listen you had better be good. If there is a rule, then that rule is: Don't be boring. None of this is easy, but if you want people to hear you, you will need first of all something you urgently wish to say, and you will need the words and the voice with which to say it. Sometimes students need to be shocked into opening their hearts and their mouths in order to find the power of speech. And here I think of my cat who was separated from her mother before she learnt to use her own voice. She had always been perfectly

mute until one day she was trapped on a balcony and I could not find her. Finally, she was so desperate that she discovered a little voice, cried out, was heard and rescued. It's a bit like that with timorous students of writing; they need to be desperate before they will dare to say what it is they need to say, before their voices will come through the fog of cliché and borrowed thoughts. The best writing is marked by the passion of urgency. You need to have some sense that you are writing to save your life. If that sounds dumb to you, then you probably don't want to or need to read on. Writers at their screens or pages are like the little cat caught on the balcony, they sometimes write best when they are creatures in danger crying out for their lives. And when I set out to trap my students on balconies, I am sometimes rewarded by the sounds of their voices.
—Carmel Bird

'I have at this moment a tremendous joy. I feel that I have found my voice, like a singer. I know I am hitting the right notes, the notes I want.'
JOHN LE CARRÉ

Letter One

SO YOU WANT TO BE AGATHA CHRISTIE

The Importance of Writing About Things You Know

'All these materials for literary work were nothing else than my past life.'
MARCEL PROUST

*D*ear Writer,
The manuscript of your short story, 'The Scream at Midnight', has been given to me for my assessment, and I have read the letter you sent with the story. You say you often feel depressed and isolated, living in a country town and taking up story writing. I can understand that. Writing is a solitary occupation at any time, and can be a lonely experience when you are the only person doing it for miles around. I'm glad you saw our advertisement in the paper, and I hope that my comments on your work will inspire you to write more. In fact the invention of stories is in itself a sort of insurance against loneliness because you can create characters with whom you become involved. Then when your work is published you will be communicating with all kinds of strangers. In *The Cinderella Complex*, Colette Dowling wrote: 'What impelled me to begin writing was that I didn't want to be alone any more.' She wasn't even talking about writing fiction; when you write fiction you have the freedom to invent a whole

world full of companions, even though you will probably, as Proust suggested, be drawing on material from your own life, in some way or other.

In the story you sent you have drawn a wonderfully promising group of characters. The busybody, Amelia, is particularly strong and interesting. I feel at once that I know her. She dominates the story, even though you have not meant her to be the main character. Why not let her be the main one? Often when a writer sets out to write a story about one thing or one character, a completely different matter or a different character starts to take control. The writer of fiction has the freedom to let the story take its own direction. However, the writer must have overall control. As you become more experienced you will be able to balance the different freedoms and controls involved in the business of writing.

'Imagination, without reality, festers.'
ANGELA CARTER

First of all I want to sum up your plot:

A group of neighbours hears a scream in the middle of the night. They all imagine something terrible has happened. However, there is a simple, sad, but funny explanation for the noise. This is not a very strong plot, and the characters are suffering from being forced into it. You seem to have thought of the plot first, and then put in the characters.

Probably no such thing as a new plot exists. Yours is not weak because it is common, it is weak because you have borrowed it. I know you didn't sit down and think: *Now which plot can I borrow today?* These borrowings come to people quite freely and unconsciously. They sneak up on you, and if you succumb to the temptation to borrow them and force them on your own writing, then the writing will suffer, the prose characters will become stiff stereotypes and, above all, the *prose* will drift into the dead and borrowed phrases and melodies of cliché. When you write fiction, there are two elements that must work together: the story and the storytelling. As you become more experienced, the beauty of this tandem operation will become clearer and easier.

> *'Fate, she said. Character is fate. Do you believe that, Mr Pigeon? Character is fate – or, if you prefer, destiny. Thomas Hardy says this, in a novel. About a man selling his wife. I have been thinking that it applies, perhaps, to houses.*
> *What do you think, Mr Pigeon?'*
> MARION HALLIGAN, 'TABORA'

Only one source is available to you for the material of your fiction. That source is your own experience, your own life, your own memory, your own dreams, and your own imagination. Even if you are writing something apparently amazing and weird and futuristic, the building blocks of it will be found deep in your own experience of the world. If you reflect on the stories of Peter Carey or H.G. Wells, you will realise that their brilliant leaps of imagination are in fact grounded in an everyday reality. They didn't stay in the everyday – neither did Proust – yet what these writers *knew* of the real world clearly nourished what they invented.

> *'The only basis for imagining people is people.'*
> SARA PARETSKY, 'MY TURN'

The busybody in your story is probably like somebody you know or used to know, and she is strong and vital in the story. Before you put another character or situation down on paper, you must examine your own memory.

—*Writing Exercise*—

I suggest you spend a few minutes recalling your early life. Remember the house where you lived when you were six. Remember the people, the food, the toys, garden, sounds, smells. Is there an incident that stands out in your memory of this time? You could continue to think quietly about the distant past and then start to *write an account* of an incident from your early life. Begin with the words:

'I remember'.

This is the first exercise I give the students who come to classes to study the writing of fiction. It is a simple enough exercise, you would think. But some people find it difficult. Some students are so frightened and shocked by what they remember and what they write and what they discover in the writing that they leave the class forever or don't come back for a long time. They come to a fiction writing class to write borrowed stories and they find the idea of discovering and exposing their own memories and feelings too much to bear. They seem to me to be thinking: 'Oh, I wanted to be Agatha Christie or Evelyn Waugh; I didn't want to be me.' The excuses they sometimes give for their disappearances from class are often interesting pieces of fiction. One student said she was leaving because she objected to the way I dressed. My clothes were too flamboyant for her, whereas another writer who was teaching a class had a student who left because she couldn't trust a man who wore brown. But many students find that this exercise sets them on a path of self-discovery that can lead them, after a period of time and a lot of work, to the creation of fiction. The lives lived by Christie and Waugh, by the way, are present in the fiction they have created.

I don't mean to suggest that all fiction is an autobiographical account of events, or even that fiction is grounded in the remembered life of the author, and even autobiographical accounts need a great deal of editing.

> *'Everyone has a history and most of it isn't very interesting. Stick to the parts that are.'*
> STEPHEN KING

Stephen King's comment can refer to characters in fiction, as well as to the life of the writer.

All I am saying at this stage is that my experience with the students has shown me that a sure approach, a fair beginning, to the creation of fiction can be made through an exploration of the life of the writer. The memory of early life is only the beginning, only an important first exercise in your development as a writer of fiction.

—*Writing Exercise*—

Another excellent exercise that never fails is to begin by writing: 'Let me tell you something about my mother.'

> *'There's a lot of people think they can take my books and analyse me from them. On that principle Agatha Christie would be a serial killer.'*
> MURIEL SPARK

To illustrate the point about finding your material within your own experience of life, here is a nice little story from *The Arabian Nights*:

> A merchant in Baghdad lived in a house with a grey marble courtyard in a cobbled street lined with palm trees.
>
> At the far end of the courtyard of the house, beneath a flowering vine, was a fountain of white

marble. One night the merchant had a dream in which he was instructed to go to Cairo to seek his fortune. So he set off. In Cairo he fell asleep in the courtyard of a mosque and was accused of breaking into the house next-door to rob it. He was put into prison where he explained to the chief of police that he had done nothing wrong but was following his dream.

'Fool,' said the chief of police, 'where has your dream got you but into prison? I had a dream. I had it three times. But I would not be so foolish as to obey it.'

'What did your dream tell you?'

'My dream told me to go to Baghdad where I would find a house with a grey marble courtyard in a cobbled street lined with palm trees. At the far end of the courtyard, beneath a flowering vine, is a fountain of white marble. Beneath the fountain there lies buried a great fortune.'

Saying nothing the merchant returned to his home, dug beneath the fountain and discovered the treasure.

I have not completely forgotten about 'The Scream at Midnight'. I have tried to demonstrate what I see to be the first error you have fallen into – that of looking for your stories in the wrong place. In a sense, your stories are inside you, and you have been looking only outside for them. You must look at your own experience for your material. The outside world will give you inspiration and ideas, but your writing will not succeed until you begin to understand that your own life is central to your work. I say 'central', and I mean only that something essential to you is the core of your writing. As you move into your work, you will find the riches of your own imagination. The memory and the imagination must both be at work. No amount of straight recollection will ultimately make powerful fiction.

Graham Swift has explained it this way:
> Deep down of course, everything a writer writes must be of and from that writer's self. But for God's sake write about what you don't know! For how else will you bring your imagination into play?

In 'The Scream at Midnight' you have made a good start, especially, as I said, with the character of Amelia. I will discuss some of the technical problems in your story next time I write. Leave that story aside for the time being and concentrate on the exercise I have suggested in this letter. Doing the exercise will have its effect on how your stories develop. I look forward to seeing more of your work.

With best wishes,

Virginia O'Day

Letter Two

'A' FOR ALIVE, 'D' FOR DEAD

THE USE OF ADVERBS AND ADJECTIVES

'When it comes to words, it's a matter of who's to be master, that's all.'
HUMPTY DUMPTY

*D*ear Writer,
I want to examine with you the first sentence of your story, 'The Scream at Midnight':

> Silvery moonlight pierced the thick green canopy formed by the branching limbs of the ancient oak trees and gently dappled the century-old marble monument that stood, forlorn and abandoned, in the remotest corner of the silent graveyard.

You have written that sentence because you want to set the scene and create the atmosphere for the story you are going to tell. You are trying to do what music does during the introduction to a film. But your sentence lacks vitality; something is holding it back from life. The life of the whole story in fact is being threatened by the adjectives (silvery, thick, green, branching, ancient, century-old, forlorn, abandoned, remotest, silent). The story is in jeopardy from the beginning because the adjectives have taken control of the writing, have obscured your vision of what you are describing.

Adjectives are like fire, good servants but bad masters. Study writers such as Vladimir Nabokov and Iris Murdoch who both have superb command of adjectives. They don't avoid them, they take control of them and revel in them:

> *'As he reached the window a long lavender-tipped flame danced up to stop him with a graceful gesture of its gloved hand.'*
> VLADIMIR NABOKOV, TRANSPARENT THINGS

> *'Up above, the neat silhouettes of roofs and the bunchy silhouettes of trees were outlined against a dark bluish sky through which the faint globe, its tail now entirely invisible, floated onward.'*
> IRIS MURDOCH, THE BLACK PRINCE

Fay Weldon has commented on adjectives thus:
> I used to implore apprentice writers to avoid adjectives, until one of them snarkily pointed out that Iris Murdoch is capable of writing sixteen adjectives in a row and it works wonderfully. A *weakness*, I now realise is nothing but a strength not properly developed.

I would still say you ought to be very careful with your adjectives for now.

Where did the adjectives at the beginning of your story come from? You borrowed them. You took them from some forgotten place and stuck them into your graveyard to try to trick the reader into thinking that you were describing something you, the narrator, remembered, knew. Readers are quite sharp, and they read your adjectives as signals of the fact that you are only *pretending* to have witnessed such a scene, in fact only pretending to have even imagined such a scene. In other words, the adjectives in your first sentence alert the reader to the fact that you cannot be trusted as a storyteller. This is a terrible thing to have happened.

If you wish to begin the story in the graveyard (and later on we will examine the wisdom of beginning in this way, in this place) you would do well, since you are not very good at imagining it, to go at night to a graveyard and then write about what you saw and heard and felt. Writing fiction can be fun. But for the time being, look at the sentence without the adjectives. Already it is stronger:

> Moonlight pierced the canopy formed by the limbs of the oak trees and dappled the marble monument that stood in the corner of the graveyard.

You will see that the adverb 'gently' has also been removed. Adverbs are sometimes even more dangerous than adjectives. The remaining words are the essential words, the ones that will convey your intention. These words, most of which are nouns and verbs, work together and let readers imagine for themselves the details contained in 'silvery', 'ancient', etc.

'Substitute damn *every time you're inclined to write* very; *your editor will delete it and the writing will be just as it should be.'*
MARK TWAIN

Perhaps you thought that you, as the writer, were the one who had to do all the imagining, and that the reader was to get every detail of the picture from your words. The reader of fiction takes pleasure in doing some of the work, and will more readily believe you and trust you if there is work to do. Strangely enough, the strength of fiction seems to lie as

'A' FOR ALIVE, 'D' FOR DEAD

much in what is left out as in what is included, as much in the spaces between the words as in the words. This is one of the strange powers at the heart of good writing. The writer's skill lies perhaps as much in creating the spaces as in finding the words to put down.

When I read a story with the aim of assessing or grading it, I think of placing it on a scale from A to D. This scale is readily understood by students. However, when these letters are applied to works of fiction, I think of them as standing for Alive and Dead. (B is nearly alive and C is nearly dead.) Dead prose is boring prose. It is unconvincing and uninteresting and more often than not it contains lots of adjectives and adverbs clinging like parasites and drinking its blood. They are filling up spaces which should have been provided for the use of the reader.

I sometimes describe strong, simple prose as 'plain vanilla' writing, whereas overwritten prose, with its burden of modifying adverbs and adjectives, is 'chocolate and pistachio'.

— *Writing Exercise* —

Take this example of plain vanilla writing by Sherwood Anderson, and rewrite it inserting some adjectives and adverbs.

> Pushing her way among the weeds, many of which were covered with blossoms, Mary found herself a seat on a rock that had been rolled against the trunk of an old apple tree. The weeds half concealed her and from the road only her head was visible. A hedge separated the orchard from the fields on the hillside. Mary intended to sit by the tree until darkness came creeping over the land, and to try to think out some plan regarding her future.

What effect have your additions had on this piece of prose? Worth noticing here is the fact that the reader is interested in this landscape and atmosphere because they are affecting the character Mary. Furthermore, this sliver of prose makes you long to know why Mary is pushing her way among the weeds, and what her future holds.

Here is a piece of overwritten prose for you to pare down by removing the unnecessary words:

> The summer-idle water mirrored the towering cliff in a tea-brown pool, and in a small low cave at the crumbling base of the cliff, the soft grey birds were huddled tightly together.

Some of the adjectives in the above sentence could be retained. Decide which ones are really useful. When an adjective or adverb is well chosen and well placed it can have a wonderful effect – as in the pieces I quoted from Nabokov and Murdoch. The writer's task is to gain control of the words, to make choices and decisions about which words will work to strengthen the writing and which will only weaken it. Another interesting thing to do with the sentence above about the birds is to rewrite it using different adjectives from those used originally. There are, after all, adjectives and adjectives.

When you are writing fiction one of your aims is to give the reader a fresh view, a new impression of things. Many nouns in English commonly attract certain adjectives. You hear of 'crumbling ruins', 'dire necessities', 'earnest wishes', 'driving rain', and 'sparkling eyes'. If you find yourself using one of these clumps of words, examine your work carefully before you allow the adjective to stay where it is. Adverbs present the same problem. Think of 'driving recklessly', 'sleeping soundly', and 'stumbling blindly'.

'A' FOR ALIVE, 'D' FOR DEAD

Now read through your story and mark all the adverbs and adjectives with a pencil. Do not use anything at this stage except a lead pencil. Challenge each word you have marked. Does it have a right to be where it is? If not, cross it out.

You have begun the process of editing and rewriting your story. This is not a sad time; it is exciting. The story will come to life as you work.

Rebecca West once rewrote a chapter twenty-six times. And so did Turgenev. Take heart.

With best wishes,

Virginia

Letter Three

TOP AND TAIL

Looking at Beginnings and Endings

'Courage is the first essential.'
Katherine Anne Porter

*D*ear Writer,

You will often hear me speak of the kinds of courage required by the task of writing. One sort of courage is that needed to take a cold look at the first and last sentences or even paragraphs of your story. Having looked at these you sometimes need the courage to delete them.

Look at your first paragraph, which is a description of the night and the graveyard, and which leads up to the scream. You will by now have decided that the scream does not need to be 'blood-curdling' and that the idea of its splitting the night like lightning brings in an unlikely image, which we could do without. My question is: *Do you need any of this first paragraph at all?* But this, you will say, is what sets the whole story off; this scream that seems to come from the graveyard in the middle of the night is what the story is all about. How can I leave it out? Why should I leave it out?

All I am suggesting at this stage is that you look at the story without that paragraph.

TOP AND TAIL

The story now begins: 'Amelia Grove sat bolt upright in her chair.' This is a much more promising beginning. I am interested in it at once. I wonder who Amelia is, why she is sitting, and what causes her to sit up suddenly. I say it is promising, but I think it could be improved. (I hear you groan.) How would it be if you just wrote: 'Amelia sat up'? How would it be if she had a name which was not so quaint? What if the first thing you wrote was: 'Barbara sat up'? Why did you want to tell the reader that her full name was Amelia Grove? You did this to let the reader know roughly the age, and a little of the personality. She is a bit of an old busybody, and the name signals some of this information.

Names must be consistent with the character's age and type up to a point, but when a writer relies heavily on the name to tell the reader what the character is like, the writer is in danger of creating a poor caricature, of becoming lazy about the real sketching of the character, and of writing a stock character. I realise that Charles Dickens was the master of the suggestive name – think of Ebenezer Scrooge and Wackford Squeers. The names were part of the comic and terrible energy of the narratives, a deep part of the creation of the characters. Somehow Dickens was able to concoct the character and the name as part of their own fabric. It is possible to do that, but my point is that 'Amelia Grove' is not really functioning for you, is not coming out of the energy of the story. Give it some thought.

At the beginning of *Jerusalem the Golden*, Margaret Drabble draws attention to the significance of the name Clara, which is the name of the principal character. 'Clara never failed to be astonished by the extraordinary felicity of her own name.' I actually find this a bit over-dramatic, suggesting as it does that Clara was always falling about in amazement at her own name, but one way to deal with the matter is to draw attention to it in some way.

The material in your first paragraph, which I suggest you abandon, is the material going through your mind when you begin to write the story. You think: 'I will set this story in a graveyard at midnight and the trees will be spooky and the tombstones will be creepy, the shadows eerie. Then a piercing scream will be heard.' You are free to think this, and you probably need to think this, but you do not need to *tell it to the reader all at once* as you have done.

> It was a Saturday night when the man with the
> red waistcoat arrived in London.
>
> PETER CAREY, JACK MAGGS (OPENING SENTENCE)

I warn my new students that when they find themselves beginning a story with the description of a scene, they need to beware in case they are boring the reader with the writer's own private thoughts on *how to begin*, how to change gear from what is called the real world to the world of fiction. The first rule of writing anything at all is not to be boring, and this gear-changing is particularly numbing for the reader.

Look at some opening sentences by some other writers who do not waste time changing gear in this way. Examine every word in these examples, observing how much key and fascinating information is contained in them, and how they insist that you read on.

> I met my husband at the airport, and there he
> told me some things that wiped the smile off my
> face.
>
> HELEN GARNER, 'MY HARD HEART'

> Our car boiled over again just after my mother
> and I crossed the Continental Divide.
>
> TOBIAS WOLFF THIS BOY'S LIFE

> The marriage wasn't going well and I decided to leave my husband.
>
> ANNE TYLER, *EARTHLY POSSESSIONS*

I chose those opening lines at random from books on the shelf next to my writing table. It so happens that all three writers have begun their stories in the first person. In my next letter I will discuss the question of whether you write a story in the first or the third person. Here is an example of the beginning of a short story written in the third person:

> The place called *Black Horse* is marked on the map but there is nothing there except a store and three houses and an old cemetery and a livery shed which belonged to a church that burned down.
>
> ALICE MUNRO, 'A TRIP TO THE COAST'

I love the way it moves from the vivid name of the town to the information about the missing church, the space which is evidence of an ancient fire. You will notice that there is really only one adjective, 'old'.

'You can't simply say to people how you begin a novel; it's like falling in love with someone slowly; you're not quite aware of when it started.'

CHRISTOPHER KOCH

Before leaving the matter of surgery for 'The Scream at Midnight', we must look at the final paragraph. The writing is much stronger, simpler and more self-assured than it was in the first paragraph, as though the story itself has given you courage and practice. But you should consider removing that final sentence: *Thank God!* she sighed at last as she gently closed the front door and stood for a long time in the darkened hallway.'

Here you have written a kind of stage direction, which is unnecessary. Try ending the story where you say: The car seemed to slow down for just a moment. Then it speeded up and was gone.

You need to be brave to remove the beginning and the ending of your story. If you are brave enough, your story will begin to change and improve. Rumer Godden said: 'It takes a lot of courage to be a writer.'

Look at this ending to Eudora Welty's story, 'A Visit of Charity':

> Marian never replied. She pushed the heavy door open into the cold air and ran down the steps. Under the prickly shrub she stooped and quickly, without being seen, retrieved a red apple she had hidden there. Her yellow hair under the white cap, her scarlet coat, her bare knees all flashed in the sunlight as she ran to meet the big bus rocketing through the street.
>
> 'Wait for me!' she shouted. As though at an imperial command, the bus ground to a stop.
>
> She jumped on and took a big bite out of the apple.

Apart from the superb way in which the whole thing leads up in crescendo to the bite of the apple, there are quite a lot of strategic adjectives used. I think you will find that they are all working, earning their place in the prose.

And here is the ending (I love this one) to *The Long Farewell* by Michael Innes:

> 'There's no moral. There's only a caution.'
> 'And that is?'

'When you're in the middle of Italy, think twice when a voice calls "Come in."'

I am sorry about all those quotation marks.
With best wishes,

Virginia

Letter Four

THE OMNISCIENT AUTHOR

Choice of Point of View

'The true artist is the person who never takes anything for granted.'
VLADIMIR NABOKOV

*D*ear Writer,
You will see that I have written the letters 'OM A' on your story. All this means is that the story is being told by an omniscient author, one who sees and knows all, and chooses to write some of it down for other people to read.

In my last letter I raised the matter of the story's point of view. The point of view also involves the narrative voice of the story.

'The Scream at Midnight' has a third person point of view, and the narrative voice is that of the omniscient author. This state of affairs is traditional, and as you are familiar with reading stories of this type, you can be expected to feel comfortable with the third person OM A. It is the voice and viewpoint of the old-fashioned storyteller – of 'once upon a time'. Beware of this feeling of comfort and ease. Because you have read so many third-person stories you may be inclined to think that the reader will automatically believe an OM A. Do not take your readers for granted in this way.

THE OMNISCIENT AUTHOR

I don't think Nabokov was thinking of this when he said artists take nothing for granted, but what he said applies here. I have said before that readers are sharp; they are also easily disgusted, insulted, put off. So your *reader* can be seen as the artist referred to in the quotation from Nabokov. At this point my students sometimes say, 'But who are all these readers? We are only writing these stories for ourselves.' I explain to them that I am unable to believe such statements. If they didn't want somebody to read their stories, why did they write them down? Is it a deep-felt desire to preserve their own time on earth? Is it a mark, like the heart with initials carved on the tree saying 'I was here'? Is it a talisman against mortality? Probably. But there is no reason why it shouldn't also be good prose. Even if nobody is going to read it.

THIRD PERSON NARRATIVE

Here are some examples of third-person narrative:

> That evening she scrambled eggs and fixed a bowl of tomato soup. Then, after putting on a flannel robe and cold-creaming her face, she propped herself up in bed with a hot water bottle under her feet. She was reading *The Times* when the doorbell rang.
>
> TRUMAN CAPOTE

> Both paused to watch a black man in white linen drawers running through the pale fields for dear life, with a large brown paper parcel in his hands.
>
> KATHERINE MANSFIELD

The writers of these two examples have fully imagined the things they are writing about so that the third person/

omniscient author technique is successful. A reader feels safe to believe what is being told because the teller believes, because the writer is in control of the material.

You have to know what you are writing about, have to believe what you are saying, have control of what you are saying, and care about it. The question of caring is an important one. If the writer does not care about the story, how can the reader be expected to care?

A writer who cares will never make the mistake of saying, for example, that the character could smell the perfume of the hydrangeas. Hydrangeas have no scent. When the reader reads a mistake like that, the reader immediately loses faith in the narrator, in the story. Every detail of your work has to be checked against the truth, however insignificant the detail may seem to be. Nabokov's words about taking nothing for granted would apply here. Take nothing for granted. Don't guess. And don't hope that nobody will notice. Somebody will notice – let the first one to notice be you, so that you can fix it up. There are famous examples of writers who have slipped up on this. Such as the mistake William Golding made with Piggy's spectacles in *Lord of the Flies*. It would not have been possible for the boys to start fires with those glasses. Because the novel is so beloved, people often say this detail doesn't really matter, but in fact it would be better if the mistake hadn't happened. Don't you think? The third person is setting himself up as an authority on the material, and even if part of his nature is that there are certain things he doesn't know, the business of getting the fire going should not really be one of those.

Writing of the French writer Robert Pinget, John Updike says that Pinget has 'a love of his material', and says that this love is one of the essential passions of a writer. If you love your material and are passionate about it, you probably won't make mistakes with its details, and furthermore, your love will be a persuasive element in your work. In my next letter, I will talk about love, passion and dedication.

One of my favourite novels is *The Great Gatsby*, and I fondly forgive Fitzgerald the odd little factual errors such as mistaking an iris for a retina, but you can't expect your readers to be as soppy as I am. And it would have been so easy for Fitzgerald to have got it right.

FIRST PERSON NARRATIVE

> In my younger and more vulnerable years my father gave me some valuable advice that I've been turning over in my mind ever since.
>
> F. SCOTT FITZGERALD, THE GREAT GATSBY

> I was a child murderer.
>
> JOYCE CAROL OATES, EXPENSIVE PEOPLE

Within the categories of first and third person narratives, there are many different approaches, but the fiction writer really has just the two broad categories to choose from. The nature of the material will determine the tone of the work, and also how close the reader feels to the narrator and to the material.

When you read the stories of other writers, notice from now on how the point of view is achieved. Virginia Woolf, in *To The Lighthouse*, uses the interior monologue, which is a type of first-person account. Writers sometimes address another person, a second person, as 'you', but they are still really telling the story in a narrative that is coming from the position of a first or third person. In these letters I am talking to you, Dear Writer, but the person telling the story is me, first person Virginia.

Reading the stories of others can be nourishing for you as a writer in several ways, but for the moment I suggest you study stories to find out the techniques used by your favourite writers to achieve the effects you would like to achieve. They are probably your favourites because they speak to you in a way that you might like to speak to others. So it is a good idea to analyse how they do what they do, and use what you discover as a guide. Never forget that reading is a key to writing. People who don't read well don't have much chance of writing well.

Nothing can replace the passionate love of your material. This love is one of the driving forces behind the work of the writers I quote in these letters. You need to read the works of well-known writers from all periods of literature, and to keep up with new work which is appearing all the time. You have to haunt bookshops and buy books. If you want to be a writer, you will want people to buy your work. It makes sense that you would buy the work of other writers. It is also a good idea to subscribe to magazines about books, and to read the book pages of the newspapers.

More important than reading other people's stories, however, is writing your own stories, practising. Perhaps finding the time to do this is not easy. I will talk about this problem of time in the next letter. On reading and writing, Roger McDonald said in an interview: 'Where reading can be a dream, writing can be a nightmare.' That's an awful thought, isn't it?

—*Writing Exercise*—
Here is a third person piece from *News of a Kidnapping* by Gabriel García Márquez.

She looked over her shoulder before getting into the car to be sure no-one was following her. It was 7:05 in the evening in Bogota. It had been dark for an hour, the Parque Nacional was not well lit, and the silhouettes of leafless trees against a sad, overcast sky seemed ghostly, but nothing appeared to be threatening. Despite her position, Maruja sat behind the driver because she always thought it was the most comfortable seat. Beatriz climbed in through the other door and sat to her right. They were almost an hour behind in their daily schedule, and both women looked tired after a soporific afternoon of three executive meetings – Maruja in particular who had given a party the night before and had slept for only three hours. She stretched out her tired legs, closed her eyes as she leaned her head against the back of the seat and gave the usual order:

'Please take us home.'

Try writing it in the first person and see what changes you would need to make. You may even find it necessary to structure it quite differently. Who are you going to be? Maruja, the driver, Beatriz, somebody else? It is worth noticing that the forlorn atmosphere is not unrelated to the atmosphere you were hoping to achieve in the first sentence of 'The Scream at Midnight'. A striking difference here is the fact that the atmosphere is secondary to the *character*, is mediated through the character. Stories are usually really about characters, and where they were and what they did and what happened next – that is what follows, what grows.

Third person and first person are the broadest of categories, and you will find within them as you write and as you examine the work of other writers several subcategories. The names and niceties of these subcategories don't really need to be defined. You can move from one point of view to another within a short space, but, as always, you must be in control, fully conscious of the effect your shifts in the point of view are going to have on the narrative.

Best wishes,

Virginia

Letter Five

GIVING UP HOUSEWORK

Dedication to the Writer's Task

'Maybe writing fiction is a vocation. Maybe it's as simple as that.'
CARRILLO MEAN

*D*ear Writer,
When you listen to professional writers speaking about their dedication to their art, you hear that these writers think of their writing as a vocation, in terms applied to religious lives and tasks. You probably think it is all very well for these successful writers to talk like that, but you can't be so dedicated. In fact, the very idea of being so dedicated can seem absurd, or at least wickedly self-indulgent when applied to yourself. If that is the way you think, you are wrong. If you are going to get 'The Scream at Midnight' finished, you will have to begin to treat your writing as the most important task in your life. Remember Rebecca West and Turgenev and their rewrites. Perhaps you are going to rewrite your story twenty-six times. Oh no! Yes. And the first step you can take is to give up nearly all the housework.

Students always think I am joking when I say give up the housework. You have the choice of a clean house or a finished story. The choice is yours. I am assuming you will make the right choice.

'If you want to create, you have to sacrifice superficiality, some security, and often your desire to be liked, to draw up your most intense insights, your most far-reaching visions.'
CLARISSA PINKOLA ESTÉS

You are well on the way to becoming unpopular with your family and friends. Some people can become fiction writers while surrounded by crying babies and vacuum cleaners and so on. They are rare, and it is safest at this stage to assume you are not one of them. You have not only to find the time away from your housework, but you have to find a place where you can work without being disturbed. If this place is near a telephone, Do Not Answer the Telephone. Your writing will soon begin to reflect your seriousness and dedication.

(**Author's Note 2013**: This direction to Writer seemed so quaint that I decided to interject at this point. Today Writer would probably be using a tablet, at the very least, and would have access to internet and mobile and text message as forms of diversion and distraction. Writers might generally need to ignore these things, although many do seem to be able to move in and out of dedication and distraction, texting and twittering and writing fiction all at the same time. I confess I do this myself. I draw the line at housework. And while I have your attention, I will tell you that I keep finding things writers have said and also written about writing, things I would like to include in the letters, but they could not have been quoted by Virginia in 1988. I wonder if this matters? The things they are saying today are in fact really no different from the things that writers used to say, but I am often beguiled by the new voices. This next one is from a tweet by Joyce Carol Oates:

> In writing, what's required is time to think, brood, revise, begin again. Shattering of concentration is deadly, yet now ubiquitous.

This is all true. You will notice that it came from twitter. The case rests. I think I will maybe insert myself into Virginia's letters occasionally so that I can share some of these lovely things with you. She wouldn't mind.)

When Truman Capote published his first novel he was twenty-four, and people were amazed that somebody so young could write so well. The author's response to this perception was to say: 'I'd been writing day in and day out for fourteen years! The novel was a satisfying conclusion to the first cycle in my development.' Fourteen years in the making.

Gerald Murnane said in an interview:

> It's an uncanny thing to me that the part of me which produced *The Plains* seemed to me to be such a small part, and as I was writing it, I seemed to be writing something that was almost wilfully eccentric as if I was saying to myself nobody will like this so I'm going to keep on writing it. It was the cry of a rat cornered in a room. And suddenly I found that was the way to write.

These writers are talking about their vocation, their dedication to write, which rules their lives, and is against common sense. This kind of dedication implies passion and faith. And I think the image of the rat cornered in the room is a telling one, as it illuminates the lonely, dangerous, sad, ugly things about writing, things that are often overlooked.

And F. Scott Fitzgerald explained to a young writer that if she wanted to succeed she would have to 'sell her heart'. It sounds so dramatic, giving up not only the housework but the rights to your own heart. But that's the way it is. Fitzgerald also said:

> The whole equipment of my life is to be a novelist. And that is attained with a tremendous nervous struggle; that is attained with a tremendous sacrifice which you make to lead any profession.

However, there is also great joy to be found in your work as a writer. In *Zen in the Art of Writing,* Ray Bradbury said:

> You must stay drunk on writing so reality cannot destroy you.

Writers are often given to the dramatic comment.

So take heart. And do give up the housework.

With all good wishes,

Virginia

Letter Six

THE NAME OF YOUR ANGEL IS DESIRE
About Writer's Block

'Seek the psychological origin of the paralysis.'
Anaïs Nin

*D*ear Writer,
Now that you have got the lawn mower and the dishes and the baby out of the way for a while, and you are sitting in your special place with your typewriter and a blank page, you have only one more obstacle. That obstacle is yourself. You are getting in your own way. You are a monster. You can't write fiction. You can't write anything. But yes you can. You can make some lists. First make a list of what you want. That will be list A. This is a short list and, to make things easier, I have done it for you. If I got it wrong, feel free to make alterations.

List A: What I want

I want to write a good story
I want to get it published

Now make a list of the problems that are getting in the way of A. Again I have done some of the work. You will have plenty to add.

List B: Problems

Lack of time
Lack of ideas
Can't think
Fear of failure
Fear of success
Don't know what a story is
Don't know how to start
Don't know how to finish
Feel foolish
Shoulders ache
Hungry
Need cup of coffee
Don't know any writers
Don't know any publishers

This list goes on forever so that B can interfere with A *forever*. B can really be summed up as anxiety and SELF-DOUBT. These are the names of your monster, anxiety and self-doubt. Their secret name is FEAR. The name of your angel is desire. Now you can leave your typewriter, leave your special place. If by any chance you have gone to a hut in the mountains to write for three days, there is no need to pack up and go home. Just go and have a sleep.

—*Writing Exercise*—
Give up and go to sleep. Do not return to the typewriter until you have had a sleep. Before going to sleep put paper and pen beside you and when you wake up, start writing immediately. Write anything. It doesn't matter what it is. You have permission to write and write and write.

This writing is done in the relaxed state after waking, before your monster has had time to gather its wits and sharpen its claws. Your angel is free to fly onto the page. Practise this kind of writing *every day* when you wake up. Every day. Yes, writing fiction will have an effect on your love life.

I have said this writing may not be anything but a practice, an exercise – but it can also have the effect of solving problems in stories you are working on. Scott Fitzgerald said, in a letter to his daughter:

> Sometimes you can lick an especially hard problem by facing it always first thing in the morning with the freshest part of your mind. This has so often worked for me that I have an uncanny faith in it.

The relaxed state after sleep is a state with which you must become familiar. It will become possible to summon this state even when you have not been sleeping. The brain may not be as fresh as the early morning brain, but it will have acquired the ability to get into the sort of meditative state you need. Some of my students find it helps to write on trains or at the beach, in places where their monsters seem to go off duty. Writing in a busy café can in fact result in easy, fluent work too.

Later on you can sometimes work with the material you have written, using it as the stuff of stories. But that is not its real importance. The real importance of this after-sleep/train/beach/café writing is that doing it gives you a chance to achieve a state of relaxation in which you can gain confidence and freedom, and in which your angel can sing.

If you are ever wondering what to write about, just go back to 'I remember …' Let the angel within tell the story of the child within. Tell them something about your mother. And also try going for a walk. There's nothing like fresh air and exercise to get your imagination going. Another thing – it is important to move back from your desk and gaze out at the horizon. This is not necessarily to give you inspiration, but to give your eyes the chance to re-adjust. And while you're at it, stand up, take some deep breaths and do a few pliés.

'I have never suffered from writer's block. This may have something to do with the muddy way I begin each chapter – a poorly typed incorrectly spelled mess of messages and questions to myself.'
PETER CAREY

Virginia Woolf wrote of the significance of recollections of early life, and of the sensations associated with these recollections. In 'A Sketch of the Past' she said:

> The peculiarity of these two strong memories is that each was very simple. I am hardly aware of myself but only of the sensation. I am only the container of the feeling of ecstasy, of the feeling of rapture.

If you have never achieved this sensation with your writing, please keep writing after sleep, keep letting your recollections of your early life take form in words. You will be rewarded, I promise. A remarkable thing about the 'I remember' exercise as I have observed it in students is that the writing is often not just lucid, vivid, musical, but in fact *perfect*. The writers are in touch with the 'sensation' of which Virginia Woolf speaks, and are the mouthpiece for the 'feeling of ecstasy'. The ecstasy really refers to the sensation of writing, not necessarily the emotions expressed in the sentences. Quite often the emotions are negative, for the memories of early joy are somehow less powerful and significant than early memories of sorrow or terror. Connection with these old emotions and the details that aroused them gives the writer abilities and powers they may not have known they had. I am not saying that you can shift immediately from memoir to fiction, only that by writing these exercises I suggest gives you practice in a movement from not-writing to writing. It also gives you access to your own best writing, something that you can call on when you are constructing fiction.

> *'I do believe that the art of fiction does deal with the world, that world which in our arrogance we call* ordinary *but that it deals with it in very special and specialised ways.'*
> JOHN BANVILLE, 'MAKING LITTLE MONSTERS WALK'

If you go back to List B you will find the word 'fear'. It seems to me from my observations of students that when they say they have 'writer's block' they have in fact come face to face, in their writing, with something they are too afraid to deal with. Saying this is not much use to them or to you. However, there is a very good exercise you can do here.

—Writing Exercise—

Take a sheet of paper and a pencil (not a typewriter, really, I mean that) and write a heading 'Fear' and then write and write as freely as possible, in any way you like, on that topic.

I have simply *never* known this to fail. I know it sounds like snake oil, but in fact it is – I grope for the opposite – maybe it's fairy dust.

> *'All that is necessary to break the spell of inertia and frustration is this: Act as if it were impossible to fail. That is the talisman, the formula, the command of*

right-about-face which turns us from failure towards success.'
DOROTHEA BRANDE, BECOMING A WRITER

Remember your beautiful angel, desire. Have a nice sleep, and keep the notebook handy by the bedside.
Best wishes,

Virginia

Letter Seven

THE CENTRE OF THE MYSTERY

Further Thoughts on the Importance of Personal Experience

'When they talk about their childhoods, writers come close to the centre of the mystery they are to themselves.'
Seamus Heaney

'Children, like animals, use all their senses to discover the world. Then artists come along and discover it the same way, all over again.'
Eudora Welty

*D*ear Writer,

I have spoken before about the importance I place on recollections of childhood in the forming of fiction, and I want now to say some more things about that.

You know that I am not suggesting you simply take autobiographical accounts of your early years and call them fiction. The straight recording of events and detailing of the world we call the real world does not necessarily make fiction. Fiction writers need to have a particular view of things. It is really this view that they are giving to their readers. The events and details go into the pattern that helps to make up the view.

Fiction writers are in the business of inventing other worlds, and in doing this they take the matter of existence and weave that matter into new patterns. The matter of your existence was new when you were very young, when you began to explore the world, the people, the ideas, the feelings. When you invent a new world you need to have the vision, mind, feelings of a child. I suggest that if you can get very close to the way you were when you were a child, you will more readily be able to see things freshly, and you will find the invention of other worlds comes quite easily to you. I even believe that it is possible for you to feel more or less exactly the way you felt as a child. I hope I am not talking in mysteries. I suggest you read Virginia Woolf's *Moments of Being* in which you will find exemplified some of the ideas I have been expressing here.

'I haven't lost my childhood and I hope I never will because it is the fount and source of my writing.'
EDNA O'BRIEN

Charles Dickens also comes to mind. Part of his genius lay in the fact that he seemed to have access to the emotional landscape of his childhood, and so was able to reconstruct, in a particularly vivid way, the world in all its freshness. It is the freshness of a child's approach to experience that you need to cultivate as a writer. I do not mean to suggest that you should write in a child-like way, but that you might do well to recall, for instance, how you felt when you first saw the sea – or an elephant – or a dentist.

A little child is a stranger in a strange land and the strangeness fills the child with wonder, joy and dread. These same qualities must be present in you, the fiction writer, when you look at the world. You will better be able to create your fiction if you can see things with the eyes and heart of a child.

Remember the exercise I suggested to you in the first letter I wrote you? You start with 'I remember' and write an account of something in your childhood.

—Writing Exercise—

Now you need to go further than you did then and deliberately search your memory for a very painful incident in your early life. Write an account of this incident. I believe that when you can examine and feel again, and, most importantly, put into words on paper, the very painful things that shaped you, you will be approaching the 'fount and source' of which Edna O'Brien speaks.

Am I saying that you should always write about pain? No. But I see that when students have written about those dreadful moments, have felt them again and described them, they have begun to be freed in some way to invent their worlds, to write their fiction. I should stress here that the ability to face the pain and write it down cannot be hurried. It comes in its own time. Remember the students who fled my class in terror when they began to see the darkness looming. But I think it is important for you to know that you need to write about the pain of early life as part of your development as a fiction writer.

Often students complain that short stories and novels are too much concerned with gloomy and even tragic events. The same can be said of the news sections of the papers and the television. People sometimes try to start newspapers that tell only good news. These papers do not last because they do not sell because they are not really very interesting. If they are good news stories of very high excitement such as a royal wedding or a moon-landing, that's another matter. Page after page of sweet everyday good news does not sell papers. Drama, people want drama. Comedy is good too.

You can call the Bible 'The Good News', but remember it is also teeming with truly terrible problems. Very little comedy. But why, say the students, whining, can't people write more about the happy, good things? Well, until there is some kind of conflict there is no story, is there? Without her problems, would anybody bother to remember Cinderella? What use is the happy ending without the sad beginning? The pretty parts of the story are dependent on the ugly parts.

In fact one of the tasks of the fiction writer (a person with a lot of jobs), is to find the correct balance between the good and the evil in the story being written. There may be no rose without thorns, but you must not forget the rose. Ever. The rose is actually the meaning of the thorns, I think. Another way of saying this is to say that when things are going along nicely, people just let them happen. But when things go wrong people want an explanation. So you start telling stories and writing stories to explain what went wrong. If there had been no serpent in Paradise, would there be a Bible to read? There would, actually. Something else would have come along.

Look at 'The Scream at Midnight'. I expect you have been wondering when we would do that. You have invented the whole story because of the idea of a sudden flaw in the perfection of the night. Remember that silvery moonlight, that thick green canopy? They took their interest, didn't they, from the fact that their peace was shattered by the scream. Remind me to say something about understatement at some stage.

Writing fiction is starting to sound pretty horrible, isn't it? First you abandon normal living, upsetting family and friends, and then you have to start feeling the way you felt when they left you at crèche at the age of two. You are right;

it is awful. But speaking of your family and so on reminds me that I should answer your question about the baby, the manuscript, and the jewels. When the house is burning down you still save the baby first, then the manuscript, then the jewels. Don't, whatever you do, forget the jewels. And see how your mind runs on drama and tragedy? And how exciting it is to have to consider the choice between the baby and etc, and how you can see and smell and hear the fire?

And don't forget that in your fiction you can burn down the house, but there will be consequences. I will come to cause and effect in my next letter. They can actually appear to be different in fiction from the way they are in life. You need to remember that fiction is not life.

Anyway, why are you doing all this to yourself? Let's come back to Seamus Heaney's words about the centre of the mystery writers are to themselves. In order to explore and explain your own mystery, you write. You write fiction. Writers really don't create fiction because they know something; they create fiction because there is something they want to find out. You need not only the eyes of a child but the curiosity of a child, and also a child's imagination. I will talk more about imagination in another letter.

For the time being, I just want to say that fiction is about something interesting that happened, and something interesting is nearly always painful in some way, even when it is funny. You only have to think of how much pain there is in stand-up comedy. Is pain the centre of the mystery?

Look at the third letter I wrote to you. The opening lines by Helen Garner, Tobias Wolff and Anne Tyler swiftly introduce the problem, the pain that is going to be explored.

> I met my husband at the airport, and there he told me some things that wiped the smile off my face.
>
> HELEN GARNER, 'MY HARD HEART'

> Our car boiled over again just after my mother and I crossed the Continental Divide.
>
> TOBIAS WOLFF, THIS BOY'S LIFE

> The marriage wasn't going well and I decided to leave my husband.
>
> ANNE TYLER, EARTHLY POSSESSIONS

By the way, you can also search these three sentences in vain for useless adjectives and adverbs. They are all so rhythmical too. Beautiful.

'A true writer's imagination is always bigger than he is, it outreaches his personality. Sometimes this can be felt palpably and thrillingly in the very act of writing, and perhaps it is for this infrequent but soaring sensation that writers, truly, write.'
GRAHAM SWIFT, 'POSTSCRIPTIVE THERAPY'.

With best wishes,

Virginia

Letter Eight

STRANGER THAN FICTION

MAKING THE READER BELIEVE THINGS

'A novelist can do anything he wants to so long as he makes people believe in it.'
GABRIEL GARCÍA MÁRQUEZ

*D*ear Writer,
My daughter had two friends. One was called Zoe White and the other was Zoe Black. A friend has a daughter called Zoe Campbell, and this Zoe has a friend called Zoe Campbell. It so happens that Zoe Campbell One has very white skin, while Zoe Campbell Two has dark brown skin. In your next letter or in a conversation you might challenge me on all this information. It sounds made up and improbable. And I would say, 'But yes, it's really true.' But supposing I were writing a piece of fiction using the names of those four girls for characters. Awkward, isn't it? I would have to work hard to make those names credible or even useful in the story. For one thing, placed alongside each other like that, they seem to have some symbolic meaning. You would imagine the writer was using them for some special, deep purpose. They are a real worry for the fiction writer, those names, when they get together like that. Can it be that a terrific number of girls in Australia are called Zoe? In life, the names are a coincidence;

in fiction, coincidence is a disaster. Truth, it seems, is sometimes stranger than fiction. Truth lacks, if you like, the shape, the design that fiction has, that fiction must, I think, have.

I sometimes write the comment 'incredible' on the stories submitted by my students. And a student then comes to me and says, 'But this really happened. It's really true. I was in the second car and it was reported in the paper.' I then explain that in that case the student has to make it *come true within the writing*.

'In real life we can have effects without causes, causes without effects. Not so in fiction.'
FAY WELDON

Perhaps Dickens was able to get away with wild coincidence, but writers today cannot expect to do so. As soon as your reader can say, 'No, I simply don't believe that', about something in your work, you have failed in your attempt to create a world of fiction. It is possible to slip a coincidence past the reader, as Fitzgerald does in *The Great Gatsby*. What are the chances that Nick Carraway would rent that house next door to Gatsby who can then rely on Nick to bring Daisy back to him? But if readers have seen through the trick you were trying to pull, they might lose interest in your plot and your characters. The fictional world has fallen apart. The reader is always wondering: 'Why is this like this? Why this, not that?' The writer has to be steps ahead, having the explanation ready. And anyway, if you have the explanation for an unusual circumstance firmly in your mind, you will be writing about things with conviction. You are in charge of your world of fiction, and you are expected to make something new, true and alive, something that will convince the reader without too much effort on the reader's part.

Hemingway speaks of the making of something 'truer than anything true'. That is your aim.

'You make something through your invention that is not a representation but a whole new thing truer than anything true and alive, and you make it alive, and if you make it well enough, you give it immortality. That is why you write.'
ERNEST HEMINGWAY

The idea of *making* something when you write fiction is also emphasised by García Márquez when he says:

The problem for every writer is credibility.
Ultimately literature is nothing but carpentry.
Writing is almost as hard as making a table.

I keep coming back to the words 'problem, difficulty, hard'. And in reply to your question about the solution to all these problems, I can only say again – I expect I have said it before – that you must truly believe in what you are writing. I mean believe passionately in the world you are inventing. Laugh and cry with the people. Perhaps here is another reason for the writer's usual need for isolation and a certain amount of solitude while writing. For I mean you will really laugh and really weep. Tears.

When you are writing as a believer in the world of the fiction, you will at times hold your breath and say: 'Oh no! Not this!' because your character will be about to do something shocking or dangerous. When you believe, there will be revelations. In a mysterious way, you will be in charge, but in charge of something that also has a life of its own.

'As clearly as I would see real children my characters stand before me in my mind's eye. The story is enacted

almost as if I had a private cinema screen there.'
ENID BLYTON

I can feel your shock at my quoting Enid Blyton. 'Nobody,' you are saying, 'ever believed Enid Blyton.' Ah, but I think *everybody* believed Enid Blyton. Everybody was bewitched. And this was because she believed in the world of her fiction, and had the freedom and the confidence, even the compulsion, to put that world on paper. We are touching here on the power and the nature of the imagination. I will talk more about the imagination in my next letter. I can't help thinking of the impending death of Tinker Bell in the play *Peter Pan*. She will die unless the audience believes in fairies. So they save her life by shouting their belief.

The stories you sent me recently, the memories of your childhood, painful and pleasant, have the quality of something that has 'stood before you in your mind's eye'. These stories are based on memory, and fiction has to acquire the same quality as memory, has to be written with the same conviction as when you write down your memories. I think I should give that statement the same importance as the quotations from other writers. So here goes:

'Fiction has to acquire the same quality as memory, has to be written with the same conviction as when you write down your memories.'
VIRGINIA O'DAY

You write down your memories and share them with a reader. Your fiction must also impart that feeling of shared experience.

You say that until you began to write about kindergarten, you had completely forgotten the time you bit the boy's leg. This behaviour of memory, the way in which incidents can leap to mind as you write, is just another demonstration of the importance of writing something even when you think you have no ideas.

> *'I realised how much there was that I didn't know I knew until I began to write, and when I began to write, it came out in a kind of involuntary way.'*
> MARY LAVIN

The incidents, the ideas seem to flow with the ink. And speaking of ink, I must some time talk about the use of pens, typewriters and word processors.

(**Author's Note 2013**: Should I get in here and start talking about tablets and smartphones and so forth? Maybe not. They will probably be out of date by the time you are reading this anyway. So not to worry.)

Writers disagree about lots of things, and one subject on which you will often find them divided is that of the autonomy of their characters. Some say characters have a life of their own, and others say this is rubbish. Josephine Hart says in 'My Waterloo' that when she was writing *Damage* she was 'lost in imaginary conversations with my characters, and indeed so overcome by their emotions that I would find myself weeping in the street'.

Now that you have decided to make some big changes to 'The Scream at Midnight', concentrating on the character of busybody Barbara and her war with the new neighbour, I will suggest an exercise.

— *Writing Exercise* —
Talk to the characters. Ask them about themselves and what is going on.

So there you will be, laughing and crying, and talking to invisible people.

Best wishes,

Virginia

Letter Nine

THE THOUGHT EXPERIMENT

THE ROLE OF THE IMAGINATION IN
THE CREATION OF FICTION

'The daydream is the basis of all fiction.'
COLIN WILSON

*D*ear Writer,
In your letter you said that 'The Scream at Midnight' was a story from your imagination, and you asked whether I thought you should abandon the imagination for the time being and concentrate on writing strictly from life. My answer is that I don't think 'The Scream at Midnight' is imagined *enough*. I think you have taken an imaginary situation (one that is easily borrowed from somewhere) and you have set it down without putting nearly enough effort into what Colin Wilson calls the 'thought-experiment' of it. He begins with the daydream. If a daydream is to become a story, become indeed literature, a lot of effort will have to go into its imagining into words. If the effort is going to be worth the trouble, the daydream needs to be something you really care about. Elizabeth Jolley said:

> The writer tries to develop the moment of truth
> with the magic of the imagination.

I keep coming back to the idea that you have to be *really interested* in the things you are writing about. Your writing will be driven by your own interest in the characters and their situations.

The worlds of the imagination are constructed from things found in the everyday world, even when the stories are wild and fantastic. *Alice's Adventures in Wonderland* is a good example of what I am saying here. The building blocks, if you like, existed in Lewis Carroll's world, but his imagination took them and played with them and voilà! Actually I think it is a good idea to read *Alice* from time to time, as a form of nourishment. Play is an important element in writing fiction too. Playing with ideas, images, characters and, above all, words. You are playing with words, which are great playthings.

The idea of learning to play the piano came to me just then. There are the notes, and there are your fingers, and in order for the 'playing' to come to anything you need to practise regularly. Yes. That's obvious. Same thing with writing, except nobody has kindly written out the notes for you. Try this:

—*Writing Exercise*—

Get a notebook, and every night write down just three things from that day, things that occur to you as interesting, arresting, important, funny, sad. The things might be a lengthy conversation overheard at the checkout, the light shining through a leaf on a plant on the window sill, the distant bark of a dog in the twilight, the opening pages of *Jane Eyre*. Anything, you see. The smell of hot cross buns. Sitting for your portrait. Arguing with friends about politics. It takes usually a short time to write these things – you are not keeping a journal in the ordinary sense (if there is an ordinary sense) here. You are deliberately picking just three things from each day to document as your construction of reality. And in this construction you may (you will) later find some of those building blocks for your imagination to work with. Memory, distant memory is one thing, and very useful to you, but this little notebook – the *Reality Notebook* – has a distinct quality that makes it very special to you as a writer. It will, for one thing, tell you, over time, about patterns in your thinking and feeling, tell you about preoccupations you might not have realised before. It is such a little task – three things a day – and I think its size and simplicity make it appealing, and, in the end, compulsive.

> *'The biggest praise for my work comes for the imagination, while the truth is that there's not a single line in all my work that does not have a basis in reality.'*
> GABRIEL GARCÍA MÁRQUEZ

For a description of the power of the imagination, you could read the sequence in *The Roots of Heaven* by Romain Gary where the French prisoners defy their German guards by imagining a woman. The guards are unable to steal from the prisoners the creation of their imaginations. The prisoners have a need to create the woman, and her 'reality' is in proportion to that need. How much of 'The Scream at Midnight' do you *need* to imagine?

If you start writing about something that really matters to you, some problem that you would like to solve with your imagination, then your imagination will start to take the building blocks of everyday reality and rearrange them for you. You have to give yourself the permission to let your imagination do that rearranging. I don't think there's any conflict between the real world (the everyday world, if you like) and the world of the imagination (the world of other possibilities). There is probably a secret longing in you for the freedom to remake your world. If you were completely satisfied with things as they are, you would probably not be writing fiction. I don't suppose you would be reading fiction either. Anyway, your imagination will let you do this rearranging in fiction so long as you nourish the fiction with healthy portions of reality. Umberto Eco and Gabriel García Márquez are both often classified as writers of 'magic realism', which is pretty fantastic in its way, so it is interesting to consider their comments about reality and the imagination.

'I like to have the scene I'm writing about in front of me when I narrate; it makes me more familiar with what's happening and helps me get inside the characters.'
UMBERTO ECO

The reality in which people live from day to day is full of restrictions and inconveniences. In dreams and daydreams and fiction you can find freedom from these restrictions, but for the dreams to be satisfying, you need to be still aware of the existence of the restrictions. How will you know you have escaped if you cannot remember your prison? What do you think?

> A prince has been travelling for three days across the desert. Finally he arrives at his father's palace where he goes up onto the battlements and stands looking at the sunset. He then sees that there are two deserts, one which is a glory to the eye, the other which is a weariness to the foot. He craves the beauty he sees, but knows that if he tries to grasp it, runs towards it, he will only get his sandals full of sand.

THE THOUGHT EXPERIMENT

'The best time to plan a book is while you're doing the dishes.'
AGATHA CHRISTIE

'Luckily, I had begun to read Borges, a writer whose work was totally different from my own. I saw how he created imaginary worlds which seemed totally real. How the fantastic could be made to seem mundane, simply through the skill of his writing.'
BRIAN MOORE

Note that phrase 'the skill of his writing'.

Although 'The Scream at Midnight' can be said to fail in imagination, it also needs more attention to the stuff of reality. In creating fiction you are trying to balance the magic of the sunset with the harshness of the sand. And in good fiction you can touch the beauty you crave (or the horror, or whatever it is you crave). So you were on the right track when you asked me about the relationship between the imaginary world and the real world in your fiction.

I speak of writing about what you care about. Quite often I find that my students are not able to make up their minds about what they care about. They are not sure what it is they want to say. I think I have pointed out before that if you are in this position the only thing to do is to begin to write in order to find out what it is you want to say. You will probably make a lot of false starts, but eventually you should be able to see what it is that concerns you, what you need to be writing about. Your *Reality Notebook* will be an invaluable tool.

'The dimensions of a work of art are seldom realised by the author until the work is accomplished. The

work is like a flowering dream. Ideas grow, budding silently, and there are a thousand illuminations coming day by day as the work progresses. A seed grows in writing as in nature. The seed of the idea is developed by both labour and the unconscious, and the struggle that goes on between them.'
CARSON MCCULLERS

—Writing Exercise—

I suggest that you collect items from newspapers. Cut out anything that catches your eye, takes your fancy. Looking through your collection of cuttings will usually reveal to you some of your principal concerns, just as your *Reality Notebook* will, and should also suggest some plots to you.

Remember that the items in the daily papers will surpass your wildest flights of the imagination. But remember, if you use a fantastic news story as the basis for a piece of fiction, you will have to find ways to make it credible within the world of fiction. (I have a habit of cutting things from papers and dropping them in a large plastic storage cube. It is fun, sometimes, to sort through the pile of things in the cube.)

In *The Private World of Georgette Heyer*, Jane Aiken Hodge writes of Heyer:

> Illustrations from magazine articles were lovingly clipped and filed, so that she could turn up pictures of six different neckcloths or six different bonnets as required.

In another letter I will talk about where ideas come from. I expect you have been wondering about that.

I like to keep you in suspense.

THE THOUGHT EXPERIMENT

With best wishes,

Virginia

P.S. Just now I was listening to the radio. I heard a reference to a story that I assume to be true. Long ago the premier of Tasmania tried to arrange to meet Hitler in order to sell him some Tasmanian apples. Stranger than fiction, isn't it? The radio can also be a wonderful source of inspiration – there is something magical about the intimacy you can feel as beautiful voices tell you things on the radio. Tasmania used to be famous for its apples.

Letter Ten

BABY'S NAME

Finding a Title for Your Story

'The magic use of words is intended as an invitation to participate.'
ANAÏS NIN

*D*ear Writer,
You say that if you have to read the title 'The Scream at Midnight' once more in my letters you will start to scream and throw things. I am inclined to agree with you. It is not a very good title. (I am trying to be polite. I actually think it is a terrible title.) Your idea of calling the story 'The Teeth' is a terrific one, and the new parts on how the busybody is so anxious about her teeth, and how the child in the park bit the other child, are vivid and interesting. This reminds me to tell you what Ford Madox Ford said about style:

> The first business of Style is to make work interesting: the second business of Style is to make work interesting: the third business of Style is to make work interesting: the fifth business of Style…

This statement has been attributed to many other writers over time, but I believe Ford wrote it first, in a letter (I think) to Joseph Conrad. The origins of it might have disappeared in the mists of time, but in any case, it's a pretty good statement of the way things are with style.

And style starts with the title of the work.

I was flicking through the daily paper and I saw an article headed 'The Ghosts of Strange Arrivals'. I found that such a boring heading I didn't even look at the article. It has something of the strain of 'The Scream at Midnight' about it, doesn't it? Or perhaps you are attracted to it. I wasn't. When I folded up the paper my eye was caught by a heading on the front page directing the reader to an article on page eleven. What caught my eye was: 'The Gold-Mad and the God-Fearing'. I turned to page eleven at once, only to discover that the article referred to was 'The Ghosts of Strange Arrivals'. Same story, different title. I still couldn't be bothered reading it because the boring title hung over it like grey dust. Reading is a tricky business, isn't it?

All writers will tell you something different about how they find the titles for their stories. There are writers who say it is very difficult to find a title, and writers who think a title is one of the easiest things to find. Titles are one of my favourite things, and they spring into my mind constantly; to me the world seems to be bristling with so many titles that there isn't enough time to write the stories to go with them. I suppose the main rule for titles is that they have to be interesting. Not boring, you see. The title is, after all, the name your story will have in the world. Publishers even talk about 'titles' rather than 'books'. The title of your creation is the first step in the *marketing* of your work. Something about the title has to tickle the reader's (buyer's) brain. The title is a signal. I sometimes think of when Alice found the 'very small cake, on which the words EAT ME were beautifully *marked in currants.*' Oh to have an imperative title marked in currants. Buy Me, Read Me – marked in currants.

Titles of two words are very nice to say, and usually have a good rhythm, and are easy to remember. The title of the novel *Monkey Grip* has, I think, got everything. Two words, good rhythm, images, suggestions, reverberations, and those nifty consonant sounds M, K, G, P. (People love saying those.)

Then there's the suggestion of a joke that always lurks in the word 'monkey', followed by the awful grab of 'grip' which is very frightening. It is of course a reference to the drug addiction of the main character. The expression comes from a method used by hunters to catch monkeys, a nasty method that shows up human beings at their worst. You have a gourd hanging from a tree. You have hollowed it out and filled it with peanuts, and have put a hole in the side, a hole big enough for a monkey to put its hand in. It samples the peanuts, then it puts its hand in and takes a big handful. But now its hand is too large to get it out of the gourd. The monkey won't open its fist. Greed has closed it in the monkey grip, and the hunter can take the monkey and kill it and eat it or whatever else. Once a dealer has a user hooked, the user can't get the hand out of the gourd.

You couldn't forget it, could you? Not quite as good as Linda Jaivin's *Eat Me* of course, but close.

Study these titles:
Vile Bodies
Jamaica Inn
'The Garden Party'
'I Only Came to Use the Phone'
Animal Farm
Wuthering Heights
'May We Borrow Your Husband?'

Expensive People
A Visit From The Goon Squad
'So Much Water So Close to Home'
If On A Winter's Night A Traveller
The Lady Who Liked Clean Restrooms

What sorts of sounds, rhythms, images, meanings do they have? Do stories with long wordy titles appeal to you? They are usually taken from the body of the story – I find them very tantalising and exciting; and they are given to short fiction more often than to novels. The marketing departments of publishing houses know that selling a novel can often depend on having a short, sharp, memorable title, so that's usually what novels have. The last two titles on the list are exceptions.

Different sorts of fiction will have different sorts of titles, although there are not strict rules about this. Have I already said that there are really no strict rules to writing fiction, anyway, apart from the one rule 'don't be boring'? The thick, popular best-seller with the shiny, slimy cover is inclined to have a one-word title so that busy travellers can rush up to airport bookstalls and cry *Crisis* or *Blood* or *Lace* or *Rape*, and get the book they want.

(**Author's Note 2013**: Even in the age of the eBook reader, and the fading of the corner bookstore, the airport bookshop seems to me to be thriving. It seems that the human desire to buy a fantasy etched on a chunky fistful of pages bound in soft card prevails in airport bookshops. I think there is some illusion of security at work, some talismanic power of the book bought at the place where the traveller is about to leave the earth for the sky. A book is such an intimate, personal, portable little thing really. It *is* magic after all.)

The more reflective reader can be attracted to titles like *To Kill a Mockingbird*, *The Handmaid's Tale* and *Midnight's Children*. *Milk* is an exception here, but see how *Milk*, although one word, is not going to be a title that competes with those other one-worders. *Juice*, yes; *Milk*, no. The *meaning* and emotional freight of the single word are pretty significant.

You are still wondering how to find your titles, aren't you? Well they should rise up to you out of your story. But even the most experienced writers often say this doesn't happen all the time, and they sometimes have terrible trouble. I think it is a matter of letting the story speak to you. Remember when you were talking to the characters and listening to them? Well, you can also talk to the whole story and ask it about the title. The story needs to be alive before it can talk. And yes, this is one of those suggestions that sound a bit nutty, but they do work. What do you think of *In Cold Blood* as a title for a novel? I realise I keep switching from stories to novels here, but you did say you were working on a novel as well as writing short stories. I think we have settled on 'The Teeth' for the time being, haven't we?

—*Writing Exercise*—

Titles are, as I said, one of my favourite things and I would be quite happy to sit here staring at my bookshelves and writing down the titles for you. However, I had better suggest that you do some work. Look at your own books and write down the titles you think are good and then those that are bad. It is important that you actually write them down. Quite often, it seems to me, writers think too much and don't use their pens and papers enough. Write the titles down and read them out aloud, and roll them round in your mind as well. Don't just think about them in a kind of abstract way. You said you read my story 'Cherie Darling and the French Eccentrics'. What did you think of the title?

I am very fond of the work of Janet Malcolm, and I particularly admire her title *The Journalist and the Murderer* because it is so very, very plain, so blunt. Of course it isn't fiction, but it could be.

At the *O'Day Manuscript Assessment Service* we offer to find titles for the nameless creations of our authors, but this service should be used only as a last resort.

Is 'Last Resort' a good title? I expect it's been used, but that is not necessarily a barrier to using it yourself.

Another naming question is that of the names of characters. These sometimes spring out at you, but occasionally you might have trouble finding the right name for one of your people. The telephone book is very handy. And books of baby names. You can also have a lot of fun with names, I think.

(***Author's Note 2013***: These days you can google names to your heart's content. And for that matter it is clear that soon phone books on paper will be a thing of the past. That's quite a nice title 'A Thing of the Past'. *À la recherche du temps perdu*, perhaps. Lacking phone books and google, Jane Austen sought names for her characters in such lists as the peerage – discovering there Emma Woodhouse and Fitzwilliam Darcy. And in *Persuasion* she gave the sailors Wentworth and Croft names from records of the aristocracy, and to members of the gentry, Carteret and Elliot, she gave names from naval indexes. Sometimes a writer must have a little fun.)

Dickens is probably the most celebrated namer of characters. One of my most treasured books is *The Dickens Dictionary* by Alex J. Philip and Laurence Gadd, which gives me the name of every character Dickens ever invented, and a little explanation of who they are, taken from the works. The naming is often very purposeful, not to say colourful and amusing. The emphasis is usually on the surname, with the first name being the less fanciful. The Chuzzlewit Family from *Martin Chuzzlewit* is 'Undoubtedly descended in a direct line from Adam and Eve'. Seth Pecksniff is an architect and land surveyor from *Martin Chuzzlewit*.

> He was a moral man, a grave man, a man of noble sentiments and speech. He was a most exemplary man: fuller of virtuous precepts than a copy-book. His hair just grizzled with an iron-grey stood bolt upright, or slightly drooped in kindred action with his heavy eyelids. His very throat was moral. You saw a good deal of it. You looked over a very low fence of white cravat – and there it lay, a valley between two jutting heights of collar, serene and whiskerless before you.

Quite often the names of your own characters will spring into your mind as you create the character and the action, and it is usually a good idea to follow your first instincts. You only have the equivalents of Pecksniffs and Chuzzlewits if you are bounding off in Dickensian comic directions, but there is always a lot of interest for a writer in marrying the character to the person in some way. Imagine calling a character 'Heathcliff'.

(***Author's Note 2013***: The Harry Potter books are rich in exciting names. Some of them – Dumbledore and Muggle – are close to names in Dickens, such as Dumbledon and Muggleton.)

BABY'S NAME

You can get a lot of pleasure from finding titles for your stories, and names for your characters. Never lose sight of the joys of writing.
With best wishes,

Virginia

Letter Eleven

CAUSE OF DEATH

Some Points to Check When Revising Stories

'Style takes its final shape more from attitudes of mind than from principles of composition.'
Strunk and White, Elements of Style

*D*ear Writer,

The underlying cause of the death of prose, or should I say that failure of prose to ever come to life, is the writer's lack of passion about the subject. However, if you identify and treat the symptoms of the disease of passionlessness, you can often awaken the passion and so revive the prose. This is a curious phenomenon. Treat the symptoms and cure the disease.

Below, I have written a terrible paragraph containing a lot of faults which I have numbered. In this paragraph these things are faults, weaknesses that let the writing down; however, there are times when these devices may be useful to the writing – it ultimately is up to you, the writer, to develop the sensitivity to your subject and your language that will tell you when, for instance, the passive voice would be better than the active. The faults here are:

    1. Cliché
    2. Jargon
    3. Pathetic fallacy

4. Passive voice
5. Mixed metaphor
6. Stilted dialogue
7. Overwriting

Here is the paragraph in question:

Outside the elegant split-level (2) mansion the dark, noble (1) pine trees stirred (3) in the sunlight, responding (2, 3) to the unseasonal (2) warmth. Then the peaceful idyll (1) was shattered (4, 7) by a sharp cry. Isabella stood stock still, (1) her dark eyes widening (1) in terror. (7) She realised then with a shock (1) that the winds of change were drawing to a close. (5) 'No matter what,' exclaimed Isabella breathlessly, (7) 'I will never leave here!' (6)

Cliché

A cliché is a tired, borrowed expression that comes very easily to the pen, and blurs the picture you are trying to create. When you put a routine adjective with a noun, for instance, you bleach the noun of its effect, whereas you were hoping to add to its power and interest. And rather than giving a noun an adjective, you could try writing a whole phrase or sentence of description, if details about the noun are so important to you. Try to think of a fresh way of achieving the effect you want. Consider this description of a wolf from *By the Shores of Silver Lake* by Laura Inglis Wilder:

> The wind stirred his fur, and the moonlight seemed to run in and out of it.

That sentence is alive, the wolf is alive, the reader is alive. The writer too, alive forever.

Jargon

It seems to me that jargon is becoming more of a problem than cliché in a lot of the writing I see. Writers describe people's lives in the words invented by social workers and psychologists so that stories are written about partners in 'relationships' having 'lifestyles'. Computer jargon is another popular one so that things other than data get 'updated' and 'interfaced'. Jargon is a way of making sure the words you are writing will obscure your meaning and keep emotion at bay.

Pathetic fallacy

When things in the natural world such as trees and fields of wheat start breathing and sighing and generally behaving like human beings, the writer is employing a device which only makes the writing ludicrous, or at best comic. There's nothing wrong with being funny, if that's your intention. Study the prose of P.G. Wodehouse for lessons in how to tickle your reader's funny bone. Dickens, too.

Passive voice

When a verb is active (Mary ate the orange) it is often stronger, more lively than when it is passive (The orange was eaten by Mary). If the matter of the orange and its fate is the key thing of interest in the narrative, than probably the passive voice is what you want, but if Mary is your subject, then give her the chance to be active.

Mixed metaphor

Metaphor is one of the most beautiful and powerful devices at the writer's command. Simply, you are writing metaphorically when you are giving the reader two unrelated images at once, blending the two to make a new image in the reader's mind. It's what poets do all the time. 'The road was a ribbon of darkness.' This is a simple example of metaphor, but great writing can subtly give metaphoric force to whole sequences. Be careful that you know exactly what you mean and follow through with your meaning. I once heard an angry woman on the radio describing herself as having become 'a fly speck on some politician's highway of life'. This is actually amusingly mixed, and I did like it, but it is probably the kind of thing to avoid in fiction – unless it is in the character's mouth, of course. That would be grand. Wodehouse might give it to a character. And quite often it is more powerful and effective to say 'He was sad' than it is to try to get your point over with a metaphor. Sinking in a sea of grief, which is of course a cliché, is much less interesting than the plain statement.

> *'Her voice was full of money.'*
> JAY GATSBY

Stilted dialogue

Dialogue is often one of the most difficult things for the new writer to create. You don't have to reproduce exactly what you have heard people saying, but you have to create the impression for the reader that the reader is listening to something which is or was being said.

—*Writing Exercise*—

Listen carefully to what people say, and then practise writing it down, practise re-creating it so that it sounds like talk. You are not taking a photograph of speech, you are creating an impressionist picture. You really will need to practise. Instead of using overwritten terms like 'exclaimed', try to keep to good old 'said'. And the more often you can omit the 'she saids' and the 'he saids', and still be sure the reader knows who is talking, the better. Do not start writing in dialect until you are very, very experienced. And even then, be very careful. Leaving out the adverbs, such as 'emphatically, miserably' is also a good idea. Try to let the conversation itself make the mood of the talk clear.

Overwriting

If you go back to the first paragraph of 'The Scream at Midnight' as it was when you first sent it to me, you will see that one of the problems with it was overwriting. You tried to engage the reader's attention by saying things were blood-curdling, splitting, piercing and so on. I just noticed that all those words were present participles being used as adjectives. Perhaps when you reach for a present participle you might pause, gaze out at the horizon, and move on.

Have a look at the sentences I quoted from Iris Murdoch and Vladimir Nabokov in Letter Two again – they are beautiful models of effective simplicity, while making use of lots of dangerous adjectives. The Nabokov quote is also an example of metaphor, and even of a kind of pathetic fallacy. But oh, the joy of it, the power of it. You see there are no rules really.

So those were some of the diseases that stories can pick up as they travel from the place of perfection in the brain of the writer, down the arm, through the pen and onto the paper. (In the next letter I must talk about this pen I keep referring to.) I didn't get any Latinisms into my awful paragraph about Isabella. (Was it about Isabella, or was it about nothing at all?) Anyway, Latinisms are another disease.

Latinisms

New writers often like to use long words, which have come into English from Latin and French, rather than the shorter, simpler words coming from Anglo-Saxon. These Latinisms can make the prose tedious and blurred and pompous.

What, for instance, does this really mean: 'A considerable element of the unpredictable must invariably be taken into account'?

Would the meaning be clearer if the words were more simple? Deep down beneath the Latinisms (and the jargon and the cliché) there is a simple English language that we all know, understand and feel. Find it for your own writing. Find it.

CAUSE OF DEATH

Abstract nouns
These nouns are the ones that name qualities rather than things. Capacity, responsibility, motivation – these words are abstract nouns, and are examples of the sorts of words people often use when they are *not* trying to express themselves clearly and precisely. If you send your child to a school that aims 'to cultivate consistency and perseverance through routine and activity, while at the same time maintaining flexibility to avoid rigidity', how do you imagine your child will spend the day?

Concrete nouns such as 'bread', 'soup', 'face', 'wood', 'hut', 'tower', convey the mental pictures with which people can imagine the worlds that fiction writers are describing. You are painting a picture, working with images that your reader can see, and there is no image for abstractions. And again, as with most so-called faults of writing, the abstract nouns have their place, and can be powerful tools of expression, provided that you are in control, that you know what you are doing and why you are doing it.

If you can avoid these common faults, your writing will say what you want it to say, do what you want it to do, and I think you will be astonished and delighted. In this letter I have not given many examples of good writing. I felt that rather than nip little pieces out of great stories for you, I should remind you that one of the jobs of the writer is to be a reader. As you read, notice the absence (or presence) of the clichés and the mixed metaphors, and discover the ways in which the writers you love are using the language you love.

Just for starters, here is a little piece of Wodehouse:

> As a writer of light fiction, I have always till now been handicapped by the fact that my disposition was cheerful, my heart intact, and my

> life unsoured. Handicapped, I say, because the public likes to feel that a writer of farcical stories is piquantly miserable in his private life, and that, if he turns out anything amusing, he does it simply in order to obtain relief from the most insupportable weight of an existence which he has long since realised to be a wash-out. Well, today I am just like that.

My favourite word in there is 'piquantly', a surprising little adverb that seems to provide the hinge for the whole paragraph.

It's worth considering the work of Wodehouse, generally, at this point. I confess he is one of my favourite writers. You will realise that his work is riddled with devices I have described as 'faults', strategies to be avoided. Yes. Well, it's a matter of *how* and *why* he is doing these things. His purpose is comic, and he can drop in a passive or a cliché or a mixed metaphor with the skill of a master chef depositing a glacé cherry on a cupcake. Knowledge, practice, flair, genius – they all help, you see. Again, one of the best things you can do for your own writing is to read and read the writing of others, such as, say, P.G. Wodehouse and James Joyce.

Another aspect of all this is the matter of control, and also of *irony*. When the writer is fully in control of what he or she is doing, like, dare I say, a great puppeteer, then an ironic gap can open up between the material and the characters, and into this glorious and delicate space comes what I can only describe as the 'mood of irony'. One of the mistresses of irony is Muriel Spark. 'Dark comedy' is one way of categorising her work – I suggest you read *The Prime of Miss Jean Brodie* to see how it's done.

CAUSE OF DEATH

> *'I've talked a lot about writing, but I don't really know what it means.'*
> MURIEL SPARK

Best wishes,

Virginia

(**Author's Note 2013**: David Foster Wallace said:
> The great thing about irony is that it splits things apart, gets up above them so we can see the flaws and the hypocrisies and duplicates.

It is worth your while at this point to read his novel *Infinite Jest*, and also Hilary Mantel's *Bring Up the Bodies*, and *Money* by Martin Amis.)

Letter Twelve

IN THE BEGINNING WAS THE QUILL

A Discussion of Pens, Typewriters and Word Processors

'As the mind works the hand moves.'
Fay Weldon

'My two fingers on a typewriter have never connected with my brain. My hand on a pen does. A fountain pen, of course. Ball-point pens are only good for filling out forms on a plane.'
Graham Greene

(**Author's Note 2013**: I considered removing this letter from the collection because the technology under discussion is obsolete. However, I decided to include it because it sits within the fabric of the historic discussion between Virginia and Writer. You might find it a bit quaint.)

*D*ear Writer,
When I was a schoolgirl I used to sit in an old graveyard and write novels in exercise books. The solitude, the atmosphere of the broken-down graves, some of them tombs that had been excavated in the hillside, the shape of the book, the texture of the paper, the black ink that flowed from the fountain pen my father gave me – these things inspired me as I wrote. I liked to feel the paper under my moving hand, to smell the ink, to watch the marks on the paper as I tried

to shape the stories in my head. Although it was not at all fashionable to wear blue jeans, I used to wear them, getting them from the boys' department of the store; and I wore a woollen tartan shirt, known these days as a flannie. It was huge, because it belonged to my father. I expect that I was in some dim way imagining an affinity with my understanding of Hemingway. Tragic. God knows what I thought I was doing. In any case, I was getting off on my own version of the trappings of being a writer, and part of that was being in the graveyard (where, by the way, I was forbidden to go) and filling the exercise book with stories. Some of the tombs had great rusted fancy iron doors that hung open on their hinges.

It was very much a matter of my whole being – or what I imagined to be my whole being – involved in the process of getting the stories into the exercise book. Nobody even read the stories. I knew I was practising for something, not yet producing anything that other people would like to read. They were, as a matter of fact, awful. But certainly, as the mind worked, the hand moved. However, it was clear to me that if I was going to get anywhere with all this I would have to get a typewriter and learn to type. So when I was seventeen I got a typewriter for my birthday, and I began sometimes to retype work from the exercise book, and sometimes to compose as I typed. It was a little manual typewriter, an Olivetti 'letter-writer', red, and I stayed with it for many years, producing pretty rough manuscripts. I taught myself to type from *Pitman's Business Typewriting* by Frederick Heelis, sixth edition 1955, reprinted 1956. It was supposed to have a 'gramophone record' with it, but I didn't get that. The correct way to sit at the machine is demonstrated by a black-and-white photograph of Miss Phyllis Drury who was the winner of the *News Chronicle* Typewriting Championship.

There are wonderful letters for the student to type out. The prose is glorious. 'Dear Sir, I am much obliged to you for allowing me to peruse the plan and draft specification of the joint garage.' That was the beginning of a letter to The Rev. Sinclair Lewis D.D. who lived at the The Vicarage, Picton, New South Wales. There are five points made, and the writer finishes by saying: 'I think if these small items receive attention, everything will be in order.' How lovely it would be to get an editor's note that ended like that.

(***Author's Note 2013***: I went online and searched for Phyllis Drury. There were quite a few. I didn't persevere, and so I didn't really locate the one who won the typing competition. She was wearing a ring on her ring finger in the picture, perhaps an engagement ring? She certainly knew how to sit up straight.)

When I became more confident and serious (I was in my thirties before this happened) I used to have my manuscripts typed by a professional typist. My first story was published when I was twenty-three, so it was done by me on the Olivetti. I wish I had a copy. Then I got a funny little electronic machine which ate up money in its demand for cartridges of ribbon, and next I got a proper electric typewriter. I stayed with that, often composing my work on it, but often also composing in a large notebook before transposing to the typewriter. I was becoming more and more confident as a writer, and I was also becoming aware of the many advantages of using a word processor. However, it wasn't until I was more or less forced by circumstances to use one that I realised how wonderfully useful they were.

Although the movement of my hand over the paper has gone, and the smell of the ink, and the sound of the pen, I am convinced that the mind and the fingers are still in tune, and I get a lot of pleasure out of using the word processor.

Once when Australian poet Fay Zwicky was writer in residence at Melbourne University, I invited her to speak to my fiction writing class. I knew that some of the students were using word processors for their work, and I asked Fay to tell us what she thought about word processors. She exploded in fierce lyrics of condemnation. At the time I was inclined to agree with her, but as you see, I have changed my mind and practice. But I should point out that I still use the large notebooks, still use pens and ink. Just because you take up a new pleasure doesn't mean you have to abandon all the old ones.

In the days when I used the typewriter I would write in a notebook and do a lot of correction by hand to the first draft, which was written on the right-hand page only so that the book balanced well on my knee and the left-hand page was free for corrections.

Usually when I had done about ten pages in the book, I would go to the typewriter and start the second draft of those pages. During this draft, some composition was done on the typewriter. Sometimes I'd make big changes at this stage, adding a lot of material, which wasn't written before. If I was writing a novel, I'd then go back to the notebook and do the next few pages in handwriting before coming back to the typewriter. So the novel would consist of a first handwritten draft and a slightly different typed draft. Then I corrected the typed draft by hand so that a third draft was created. Then I'd type it all again, making more changes. This draft was then corrected by hand and so it went on until I was satisfied with a final draft.

(***Author's Note 2013***: What a lot of work writers used to do. Writing novels on twitter was never like this. I did warn you that Letter Twelve was all a bit quaint.)

Before I began using the word processor, I began sending my manuscripts out to be put on disk. Then I started to catch up and now I do it myself.

I think that writing is a long slow process, and I doubt whether there are many good short cuts. The use of the word processor is not really a short cut to the writing – it speeds up much of the process of production, and facilitates storage.

Does the use of a word processor change the way you write? I don't think it has changed the way I write, but some people have told me they felt they had been taken over by the computer and were no longer in control of their work the way they used to be. One time, when I was a writer in residence at a college in Florida, I was asked by the students, who were young people who had always kept their journals on their computers, if I would teach them how to keep journals in exercise books. All they really needed was courage – the reverse of the courage I needed to get going with a word processor. Some of them also needed to be taught how to write legibly by hand. Does this matter? Is this sinister? I am inclined to think that just as our bodies need exercise – and for this they have invented the gym – we need to keep our hand in with pen and paper. Perhaps I'm wrong and just sentimental.As far as the use of technology goes, I think the most important thing is that you should be comfortable with what you are using. The important thing is to get the work done. Somehow.

With best wishes,

Virginia

Letter Thirteen

DEAR DIARY

Keeping Journals, Notebooks, Scrapbooks

'People who turn to the diary are seeking themselves, the tracing of a route toward expansion and awareness, the road to creativity.'
Anaïs Nin

(***Author's Note 2013***: Today there is a great deal of journal writing online, in myriad forms. I wonder what Virginia might have made of that.)

*D*ear Writer,
In my last letter I mentioned the large notebook in which I sometimes write, and said I would talk about keeping a journal which is a kind of letter from yourself to yourself and is a perfect exercise for a writer of fiction. Nearly every writer I have talked to speaks of keeping some kind of journal, diary or notebook as well as a file of clippings and items of interest. I think you should make some time every day to take some notes on what you have been doing, thinking, feeling. Jot down impressions you have had that day, as well as memories, dreams – everything. From such material will grow the ideas for your fiction. Stephen King tells the story of how he fell asleep on a plane and dreamt the central idea for *Misery*, wrote it on a cocktail napkin, and later developed

that whole amazing novel. The name of the pig, Misery, was in the dream.

You will begin to see the patterns in your life, see the connections between things that seemed to be unrelated. I have spoken before about writing freely first thing after rest, sleep or meditation. All this writing should be kept in notebooks. Perhaps you will never refer to it once it is written down but in the act of writing you will discover new directions of thought and feeling. I have also talked about the idea of writing notes as soon as you wake up from sleep. And in Letter Nine I suggested you write down three vivid details from the day before you go to sleep at night. Yes, there seem to be quite a few ways of keeping notes that will be useful for writing fiction. You realise you don't have to follow all my suggestions. But some, some would be good.

Returning to the idea of the word processor, there are plenty of people who keep these regular, constant notes on a computer. One man I know is recording his dreams on a computer.

I have a diary in which I record things daily, and I also make many, many notes in big notebooks. And in the big notebooks I also paste cuttings from newspapers. You can think of these as cuttings taken from somebody else's garden, if you like. They sometimes take root in the notebook and grow into marvellous hybrids with much mutation and metamorphosis. Do I sound as though I read a lot of newspapers? In fact I don't read them very often, but people save clippings for me, or tell me to be sure I don't miss something. I also enjoy the randomness of finding interesting facts and stories in the magazines I read at the hairdresser's and the dentist's. And yes, I do occasionally remove bits from these magazines and paste them in my notebook. I make notes

from books I am reading. I do read quite a lot of books. Many of the quotations I have included in my letters to you have been copied from books into my notebook. Then there is the big plastic cube into which I toss interesting bits from papers and so on that I read. I also have filing cabinets. You can work out your own methods for these things, and for how you manage your work as you go along.
(***Author's Note 2013***: Poor Virginia, poor Writer, how they would have loved google.)

> *'I use the blackboard for larger-scale projects like a film script or a book that's almost finished, where all the parts are coming together.'*
> FRANK MOORHOUSE

A word of warning here about journals and notebooks – take care you don't get so carried away with making notes that you never write any fiction.

Sometimes you will need to do a lot of research for a story you are writing – working in libraries, taking notes – oh but never lose sight of your goal, which is to write fiction, to take the experience of life and transform it, as if by magic, into fiction. In my study I have more plastic cubes in which I keep different projects separate from each other, and I think of them as containers of bits of magic – a fanciful thought, but you can forgive me. I *love* this quotation from Henry James:

> Experience is never limited, and it is never complete; it is an immense sensibility, a kind of huge spider-web of the finest silken threads suspended in the chamber of consciousness, and catching every air-borne particle in its tissue.

When you begin to keep a journal, you begin to pay a great deal of attention to yourself and to what goes on in your heart, in your strangest, most secret self. It is from this activity deep inside you that the life, the vitality, the meaning of your fiction will come. I have spoken before about the need for passion, for conviction. The journal can nourish the passion, sharpen the conviction. It can be one of your most useful tools. But, just as with the question of whether you use a pen or a word processor, the main aim is for you to find a tool that is useful to you. If you don't find the journal helpful, don't keep one. Some writers keep a special diary in which they record only their dreams. A record of your dreams can be a rich source for your work. It is the story of part of your inner realities, and from it you may in time be able to fashion a world of fiction. The retelling of dreams, your own or those of your characters, is not always successful in fiction. Watch out for that.

'Many of the most important things, I find, are the ones learnt in your sleep.'
RENATA ADLER

I have said earlier that simple retelling of childhood memories will not necessarily make good fiction. The same principle applies here. I am not suggesting that your fiction will be just a retelling of your dreams. I mean that by remembering, recording, revising your dreams you will become gradually more familiar and confident with the nature of your own passions and obsessions. Sometimes a story will be given whole to a writer in a dream, but not often. Sometimes problems that have come up in the fiction will be solved in a dream. As with looking into the truth about childhood, looking into the truth about dreams can be very frightening.

DEAR DIARY

I do not mean to suggest that you should 'understand' or try to 'analyse' your dreams. Quite the opposite really. I mean just listen to them. You will find yourself looking into a snake pit, talking to Napoleon, running naked across the stage at the opera house in Milan. You may be shaken by the violence you discover in yourself; you may be astonished by the beauty. You will certainly be gifted with the revelation of mystery. Your fiction will be enriched.

> *'I began keeping a formal journal several years ago. It resembles a sort of ongoing letter to myself, mainly about literary matters. What interests me in the process of my own experience is the wide range of my feelings.'*
> JOYCE CAROL OATES, PARIS REVIEW 1978

With all good wishes,

Virginia

Letter Fourteen

PRACTICAL MATTERS

Becoming Familiar With the Everyday World of Writing

'On a long journey carry typewriter paper and a portable machine, and make the most of your time.'
Dorothea Brande, Becoming a Writer

*D*ear Writer,
In the last letter I wrote to you I ended up talking about dreams and the mysterious side of writing fiction. I thought the time had come for me to say something about the more mundane, practical side. There really is a world of writing and writers, and you need to become familiar with it. Students sometimes come to class expecting to be given a prescription for writing fiction. The secret. No such thing exists. You become a writer by desire, dedication, practice and perseverance. However, by connecting with what I'm calling the world of writing you can be more or less always connected with what writing is about, and how it works. Read book reviews – and of course, as always, read books. Maybe join a writers' organisation, or a writing group. Go to festivals where you can not only hear what writers think and do, but you can mingle with writers, agents, publishers. There are more and more courses in writing available in places from community houses to universities. In the United States there have been places such as the Iowa Writers' Work-

PRACTICAL MATTERS

shop for many years, and in East Anglia the university runs courses. There are now many workshops appearing in other places. From information available from the University of East Anglia in 1984:

> The teaching of Creative Writing began in 1970 when the novelists Malcolm Bradbury and Angus Wilson established the first (and still the most prestigious) MA in Creative Writing, which is taught only by experienced writers with established reputations. Each of UEA's Creative Writing courses is best seen as an opportunity to explore and develop literary intentions in relation to the wider social and literary context, to work under the pressure of deadlines, and to share the experience of writing with colleagues in a critical and creative atmosphere.

The world of writing is becoming more complex and more exciting all the time, so you need to be alert to what might be offered in your own area. You can start something yourself, you know. You might be surprised how much interest there is.

(***Author's Note 2013***: How right Virginia was. The 'world of writing' as she calls it has exploded. Yet many of her suggestions hold good. Back in Virginia and Writer land you read reviews in newspapers and magazines, media that are now disappearing, their pages taking wing and flying away into the distance while their material burgeons more or less out of control online. Writer would almost certainly have a blog, I think. Somewhere somebody invented the term 'creative writing'. I am not really sure what it means, but you see it everywhere.)

Some of these suggestions sound so obvious, don't they? I am always surprised by the small number of would-be writers who do any, let alone all of these things. When you do them you feel as if you are in touch with writing. What your manuscript needs is a reader, an audience, and by getting in touch with the world of fiction, you have a better chance of finding that audience. Your stories are in a sense not really complete until someone has read them. The reader is an essential part of the contract. If you have a masterpiece handwritten in green ink in a drawer, lurking beneath tangles of string and bundles of wrapping paper and rusty pairs of scissors and the bodies of silverfish, your work is not completed. The finishing touch will be provided only by the reader. And the reader is part of that world of writing of which you need to become a part.
With best wishes,

Virginia

Letter Fifteen

WRITERS ARE DIFFERENT

A Way of Life

'What does one do at a quarter to twelve when one isn't working? I've forgotten.'
JEAN COCTEAU

'So great was the noise during the day that I used to lie awake at night listening to the silence. Eventually, I fell asleep contented and filled with the soundlessness, but while I was awake I enjoyed the experience of darkness, thought, memory, sweet anticipations.'
MURIEL SPARK, A FAR CRY FROM KENSINGTON (FICTION)

*D*ear Writer,
Yes, as you say, if you attend to all the practical matters in my last letter, you will be a very busy woman indeed. Is it ever possible to be a writer and have a job? you ask. Yes it is. But not if the job absorbs too much of you. Chekhov was a doctor of medicine – so it is possible to have a highly responsible and demanding profession and still write fiction.

'Medicine is my lawful wife and literature my mistress; when I get tired of one, I spend the night with the other.'
ANTON CHEKHOV

That's a nice way to look at it.

'I am a person with two professions. For one part of the year I am a full-time writer, working as a novelist, critic and television playwright, and earning my way in the writers' market-place. For another part I am a university professor, teaching the novel and theory, Dickens and Derrida, and making my way in the campus market-place.'
MALCOLM BRADBURY, 'GRACEFUL COMBINATIONS'

And Anthony Trollope famously worked in the Post Office, devoting the first two and a half hours of every day to writing fiction.

But if your job takes over you won't be writing fiction. If you can get a job related to writing fiction, good. But some writers prefer to have jobs that have nothing whatsoever to do with writing – jobs that take their minds off the problems of writing books. But the real point is that the fiction writer has to be *wholehearted in the desire* to write. You have to look honestly at the things that are stopping you from writing, and see whether they are stopping you because you really want to be stopped. Do you really want to write fiction? This is a harsh question, but one that probably should be asked more often than it is.

'My first wife thought the fact that I was writing was anti-family, which of course it was, it's anti-everything – the writing comes first.'
JOHN LE CARRÉ

I often hear people, even writers, say that writers are no different from other people. In most ways of course they are no different; in one way they are. Writers are the ones who write. If you are not writing you are not a writer. You are not a writer if you just think about writing. You are not a writer until you are putting words on paper. Black on white. This is work. Even when you are writing fiction, creating another world, drawing on your own inner world, you are still a real person in the real world doing real work: the real work of writing. You need, in fact, to maintain a day-to-day attention to reality and to the responsibility involved in being alive and in being who you are. Does that sound odd coming from me? I have, after all, spoken of dreams and imaginings and solitude and peace. But attention to these things does not release you from the fact that you are human. I am really pointing out that you give up the chance to work creatively if you become a slave to the distractions of everyday life. There are times when the demands of your family or other matters will dominate your life, and at these times you have to just let the writing go, put it on hold and come back to it when the time is right. Although you are possessed by the demon of writing, you still need to exercise some common sense.

But many of the would-be writers I talk to reveal that they willingly let trivial details stop them from writing. When this happens they start to complain that it is impossible for them to find the place, peace, etc to write. They are in fact not devoted to writing at all; they are devoted to complaining. I hear quite a bit of whingeing and whining. If circumstances get in their way, they can then put off writing, can blame other people, luck, and so on, can feel guilty. Then they can suffer from angry, aimless frustration which leads in turn to depression in which state they are unable to write. They are paralysed. This is possibly a form of writer's block.

You may think I am being harsh, but I see this pattern at work over and over again in people who say they want to write but can't write. They wish to write but are not prepared to undertake the responsibility that writing entails. As these would-be writers talk, I can hear the fairy tale character waiting for outside magic. In fairy tales it often comes; not so often in real life.

To get past all these problems will take courage. I haven't spoken about courage for a while.

'I tell my students there is such a thing as writer's block *and they should respect it. You shouldn't write through it. It's blocked because it ought to be blocked, because you haven't got it right now.'*
TONI MORRISON

Sometimes, Writer, I think that courage is the only thing you need. Courage to develop painstakingly from within yourself the ability to write fiction. Courage to submit what you have written to public scrutiny. Courage to keep on writing. Courage to give up housework, give up social life, give up the things that are stopping you from writing.

Am I starting to sound pious and gloomy? Writing fiction is exhilarating as you know. The fruits of passionate single-mindedness are juicy fruits indeed. The dangers are in proportion to the rewards. If you want safety and freedom from danger, don't whatever you do start writing fiction.

'There is nothing to writing. All you do is sit down at a typewriter and bleed.'
ERNEST HEMINGWAY

It is worth remembering that you can concentrate on writing fiction at one time in your life while at another

you might prefer to concentrate on working at some other demanding job – being a barrister, raising children.
Best wishes,

Virginia

Letter Sixteen

PEPPER AND SALT

Overstatement and Understatement

'It is seldom advisable to tell all.'
Strunk and White, *The Elements of Style*

*D*ear Writer,
One of the most useful and powerful devices for the writer of fiction is the device of understatement. You tell the reader less so that the reader knows more. Instead of having everything spelt out, the reader is given, in a very careful way, just enough information, for the reader's mind, the reader's imagination, to go to work. From understatement the reader can derive great pleasure and satisfaction. In popular fiction (with those thrilling one-word titles we looked at in Letter Ten) and in romantic fiction, for instance, understatement is almost never used. This kind of fiction is really an exercise in overstatement. I will give you an example of overstatement from a romantic novel, and then two examples of understatement from works of serious fiction. All three pieces of writing are meant to give the reader an image of a man and a woman embracing. The images in the second and third ('literary') examples are achieved only in the mind of the reader, whereas in the first one the romantic writer explains

things graphically for the reader. Many readers love this kind of writing. How you do things depends on what effect you are aiming for. I generally prefer understatement myself.

OVERSTATEMENT

> He advanced towards her with a purposeful expression, and she backed away, laughing, trying without success to ward him off with her hands. He caught her to him and kissed her, bending her dramatically over his arm like a twenties film heroine, and exploring her lips unmercifully until she could do nothing but wind her arms around his neck and kiss him back.
>
> *Daphne Clair*

UNDERSTATEMENT

> And by the harbour, in the midst of the wagons and barrels, at every street corner, the citizens opened their eyes wide in amazement at the spectacle, so extraordinary in a provincial town, of a carriage with drawn blinds, continually reappearing, sealed tighter than a tomb and being buffeted about like a ship at sea. Once, in the middle of the day, when they were right out in the country and the sun was beating down at its fiercest on the old silver-plated carriage-lamps, an ungloved hand stole out beneath the little yellow canvas blinds and tossed away some scraps of paper, which were carried off on the wind and landed like white butterflies in a field of red clover in full bloom. At about six o'clock the cab drew up in a side-street in the Beauvoisine quarter, and a woman got out; she

walked away with her veil lowered, and without a backward glance.
GUSTAVE FLAUBERT

In town, the lights were going on, and we were sitting on the bank on the other side of the river, and we were full of what they call love, that rough discovering and seeking of each other, that sharp *taste of one another – you know, love.*
ITALO CALVINO

Of the quotation from *Madame Bovary*, I think it is fair to say that once you have read it you will *never forget it*. The imagery is so vivid and sexual, and your imagination is given the chance to see what is going on inside the carriage without your being told about who did what to whom.

'Don't tell me the moon is shining; show me the glint of light on broken glass.'
ANTON CHEKHOV

If you take from 'The Teeth' the part where the child's mother meets the headmaster for the first time, and rewrite it in two ways, using first overstatement and then understatement, you will see how dramatically the use of understatement can affect your work. You could try showing the two versions to your potential readers to see how each version is received. Don't be surprised if people seem to prefer the overstated version. Reading understatement requires the reader to do more work than reading overstatement. It depends on which kind of readers you are looking for, but it also depends on what kind of stories you want to write, and what kind of stories you enjoy reading most yourself. Pepper or salt, herbs or garlic, adjectives, adverbs – just enough of whatever it is

– is enough. You can often find a lot of sloppy adjectives in overwritten fiction – and readers often like them, of course.

Speaking of readers, I need to say something at this point about showing your unfinished work to other people.

I will begin by warning you of possible dangers.

As a general rule, if you can possibly bear it, do not show your work to anybody until you are very confident about it. Writers are often tempted to show unfinished work to family and friends and fellow writers. More often than not (remember there are no rules) these people are a very bad choice. It is difficult (probably impossible) for anybody to be objective about reading unfinished fiction, but the people who find it hardest to be objective are your family and friends. Over and over again, although they have been warned, my students show their half-finished work to their husbands and wives and then come to me in tears and rage and tell the tale of how their loved ones rejected their creation. These people have come to know you as an ordinary member of their circle, but suddenly here you are producing fiction, using heaven knows what details of their lives as your inspiration. Fiction writers are after all cunning and cold-hearted creatures who plot and plan and creep about stealing from wherever they like. Your family readers *might* be pleased; they might be afraid – in any case their minds probably will not be clear enough for them to read your work objectively and to comment on it fairly. Your mother will either say everything you write is fantastic, or she will say something critical that hurts you. She doesn't know how to respond; it's really quite hard for her. You'll both get into some awful tangle of some kind. Dear Writer, You Have Been Warned. 'But,' you say, 'my lovers are different. They would never be unkind about my work.' Try them.

'My father, especially, was torn between exultant pride that I'd published a book and sheer horror at what was in it.'
IAN McEWAN

You chose to send your story to me for assessment. I am a stranger whose job it is to read and comment on fiction. We have a professional arrangement. If you don't like what I do you can end the arrangement without getting hurt (or not very).

You can also safely show your work to a teacher whose job it is to comment on your fiction. And there are plenty of successful writers who will tell you that their husbands or wives etc are their best critics. While that is so, the general rule is:

> DO WHATEVER YOU LIKE WITH YOUR FAMILY AND FRIENDS BUT DON'T SHOW THEM YOUR UNFINISHED FICTION.

(**Author's Note 2013**: The internet gives writers the opportunity to share their fledgling manuscripts with everybody on the planet. You can always try that if it appeals to you.)

You will find that even when your stories appear in *Vogue* and *The New Yorker*, the people closest to you will have the power to diminish your joy, but by then, of course, it will fortunately be too late.

Best wishes,

Virginia

Letter Seventeen

GETTING INTO PRINT

WHEN YOUR WORK IS PUBLISHED

'I spent that day of publication of my first book in a dream of pleasure.'
ENID BAGNOLD

*D*ear Writer,

I think Enid Bagnold's feelings on the day of publication are pretty much those of most writers. 'A dream of pleasure.'

It can be a long long time from your first thoughts about a story or book to that blissful day. *The Tale of Peter Rabbit* by Beatrix Potter was rejected by seven publishers. And in fact seven isn't really all that many in this business. Beatrix Potter published it herself, and then it was published by Frederick Warne. Such was Beatrix Potter's faith in her work that she was not discouraged by rejection but persevered in her determination to see her story published. You as a fiction writer need to have a similar faith in your work. I hope you will not find your novel or stories rejected seven times. However, I think you must realise that your book could be turned down by one or two publishers (or, to be realistic, by twenty-two) and you must remain firm in your belief in your work, continuing to submit it if it is not at first successful. I mean to encourage you, and yet here I am telling you that even *Peter Rabbit* was consistently rejected. I refrained from telling you that James Joyce submitted *Dubliners* to twenty-two publishers who all rejected it. Actually, I do find stories like that quite encouraging, although I suppose they suggest there are unpublished treasures that will never be read. I daresay there are. But I see in these stories the triumph of the determined author, and I see that triumph as an inspiration to other writers seeking a publisher. Jessica Anderson sent *Tirra Lirra by the River* to some incredible number of publishers before it was accepted. Take heart.

'I discovered that rejections are not altogether a bad thing. They teach a writer to rely on his own judgment and to say in his heart of hearts, "To hell with you." '

SAUL BELLOW

(**Author's Note 2013**: I have left the following piece of advice about finding a market for stories in the text. Apart from being a quaint old list that will make a reader smile, like when you read the instructions for darning a sock or starching a tablecloth, it does contain the essence of the process.)

As a short story writer who has not as yet had any work published, the usual course for you to follow is:

> 1. Submit your stories to literary magazines. (Try to afford the cost of subscribing to some of the magazines. It is only really by receiving subscriptions that these magazines exist at all.)
> 2. Enter your work in competitions. (You can find out about these by reading the newsletters of the writers' organisations you have joined.)
> 3. Perhaps you could read your stories in public. There are many events where you can do this;

you just need to get into contact with that world of writing I wrote about earlier.

4. Contact local radio stations and ask whether you can read your work on radio. Community radio stations in particular sometimes welcome writers who will read their own stories.

5. When you have a collection of about twenty good stories you will need to assemble them so that they are not just a random gathering of unrelated prose, but have a purpose, shape and meaning as a collection. Have a look at some recent collections of short fiction with this idea of a 'collection' in mind.

6. Choose a publisher who seems to you to be interested in publishing the kind of work you are doing, and send your manuscript to that publisher. Often publishers are more interested in publishing novels than in doing collections of short fiction from an unknown writer. But if they like the collection you send, they might be interested in talking to you about whether you have a novel nearly ready to send to them. After publishing a first novel, they will sometimes publish the collection of stories. They find collections more difficult to sell – it is easier to promote one exciting story to the reading public than it is to explain to the readers what they can expect from a collection of stories.

I have said that the course I describe is the usual course to be followed. You may proceed in your own way, but the six points I have given you can be a guide. You will realise that following those six points will take a long time. There are, as I have said before, not really any short cuts to becoming a fiction writer. Sometimes a wonderful writer seems to appear out of nowhere, but they do not, in fact, come from nowhere; they have always been slogging away at the thing for some time.

I think that the hardest step for the new writer is the first one I have listed: submit your stories to magazines. When I talk to my students I realise that a kind of emotional gulf exists between the work in manuscript and the work in published form. Sometimes I think that my main task with the students is to help them somehow to build a bridge over that emotional gulf. By an act of the imagination and by an act of faith they must step from being unpublished to being published. And these things take courage, confidence and time. Especially time. And patience.

You asked me whether I would suggest getting an agent. Agents find markets for your work and also handle the money, taking a percentage of whatever you earn. Having a really good agent possibly saves you some time and trouble, but I must stress the words 'really good'. There are publishers who won't look at anything that doesn't come from an agent. Your agent can usually present and promote your case more confidently and aggressively than you can yourself.

(***Author's Note 2013***: It seems to me that the ways a writer can have their work read these days are so much easier to access than they were in 1988. But I think it is just as hard, and yet no harder, to get a book published. There are many many more routes to publication than there used to be; it's harder to describe them, and they multiply all the time. Even the story of how the *Harry Potter* books found their way to publication is old-fashioned now; the story of today is that of the publication of *Fifty Shades of Grey* – from self-published ebook to the best seller of all time. Whatever next?)

> *'It took my agent, Christopher, a year to find a publisher. Many of them turned it down. Then finally in August of 1996, Christopher called to let me know that he had an offer from Bloomsbury. I couldn't believe my ears. After I had hung up, I screamed and jumped into the air.'*
> J.K. ROWLING, INTERVIEW IN HILARY MAGAZINE

Best wishes,

Virginia

Letter Eighteen

THE MANUSCRIPT

Preparation and Submission

'I have never finished reading your MS. It's your handwriting, you know. Perfectly legible, but so tedious.'
From an editor to D.H. Lawrence

'Many thanks for submitting your story to our magazine. You are the worst writer we've ever seen. Leave us alone. Drop dead. Get lost.'
Letter received by Snoopy in a Charles Schulz cartoon

*D*ear Writer,
Imagine you are the fiction editor of a magazine. You receive two envelopes in the mail. Each envelope contains the manuscript of a short story. You have never read any work by either of the writers, and you have never heard of either of them. One manuscript is on thin paper, folded up in a small envelope. You can see where this is going. This manuscript is faintly typed with narrow margins and spelling mistakes and corrections in various coloured inks. As I describe it I am becoming rather fond of it, as one might be fond of a naughty child. It is typed on both sides of the page. Ah but no, I hate it now. It is accompanied by a letter from the author who lists the thirteen magazines in which her stories have been published. She does not enclose a stamped envelope addressed to herself.

THE MANUSCRIPT

The other manuscript is flat in an envelope the same size as the pages, which are thick white A4. The first page is a cover page with the title of the story and the author's name and address. The text is clearly typed, double-spaced, with generous margins and no corrections. It is a clean print or photocopy. It looks very inviting. It is typed on one side of the page only. The pages are numbered. With it is an envelope with a stamp and the author's address. The author has written you a short note saying she is submitting the story for your consideration, and makes no mention of any other magazines.

Even if the scruffy one is a better piece of writing, the virtuous one has a better chance of being read, if not more sympathetically, then at least first. I might have added that the virtuous one was secured with a benign paper clip whereas the other one was pinned together with a dangerous little pin. Sometimes, you know, they come with needles. When you submit a manuscript to an editor, be sure you are giving your work the best chance by presenting it as well as you can. If you have not heard from the editor within three months, you should get in touch and ask politely about your manuscript.

The point here really is that you want another human being to *read* the thing; you should really give them a chance, do them the courtesy of making the job as reasonable as you can. I have a friend who is a great traveller. She sends me beautiful postcards from all over the world. However, her handwriting is illegible, so I never know what she is trying to tell me, but I do enjoy the pictures. It is quite interesting that the editor could read D.H. Lawrence's handwriting, but because he didn't like it, he found the exercise tedious. You'd think D.H. could have used a typewriter. I don't know.

Keep your original manuscript, and keep a record of where you sent the story. You are at liberty to send a story to more than one place at a time. If somebody accepts it, then you just withdraw it from the others. If a story is rejected, read it critically when it is returned to you, and if you still feel that it is ready for publication, send it somewhere else.

If you are submitting a manuscript to a publishing house rather than to a magazine, the procedure is the same for preparation and submission.

'I wish there were an audience for a book of this kind. But there isn't. It won't sell.'
FROM ONE OF TWELVE PUBLISHERS WHO REJECTED THE FOUNTAINHEAD BY AYN RAND

I should say something more here about rejection. I sometimes hear students telling each other, by way of consolation, that the rejection slip is a rejection of the story, not of the writer. I dispute that. I say there is no way round the writer's feeling of personal rejection. Your creation is rejected; you feel rejected; you are rejected. I think it is worth facing this fact rather than trying to pretend it isn't a fact. You have been rejected, but you believe in yourself and what you are doing. So you go on. You rewrite, perhaps; you send the work out again. You are systematic and you persevere.

'I take rejection as someone blowing a bugle in my ear to wake me up and get going, rather than retreat.'
SYLVESTER STALLONE

Good luck and best wishes,

Virginia

THE MANUSCRIPT

(***Author's Note 2013***: Even today some magazines that still publish in hard copy want you to send your work in hard copy. So what Virginia says about presentation holds good. Many places want you to send the work electronically, and they have their rules for this on their websites. Some magazines will let you know they have received your manuscript, and some will send you a rejection in due course – it can take up to a year. It is quite usual these days for editors who don't want your work to ignore your submission entirely. Take this as rejection, but remember Sylvester Stallone. Publishing houses also have their rules, and they too might ignore you. Maybe they don't have enough staff to deal with the flood of submissions. Having an agent can help, but agents don't usually deal with single stories sent to magazines.)

Letter Nineteen

SOURCES OF INSPIRATION

Where Ideas Come From

'The important thing is to find the message which liberates, unleashes one's unconscious responses.'
ANAÏS NIN

*D*ear Writer,
At last, at last, a note on where writers get their ideas.

Perhaps in desperation you asked me in your last letter to say something about inspiration, about where the ideas for fiction come from. At the risk of sounding quite hard to get on with, I'll say that the fiction writer has so many ideas, so much inspiration, that the problem is one of choice. Which ideas are you going to choose to talk about? Have I sidestepped the question? Have I not said where the ideas come from, these ideas that jostle for the writer's attention?

Anaïs Nin's words at the top of this letter are a fancy way of saying that you've got interests and ideas, and you just need the courage to get them into shape and express them. That's what it is you know. Anyhow, I will continue to discuss the matter of where ideas come from, but it really is much more simple than you think. I imagine you are perfectly capable of making up a story about why you don't need to go to the local school concert, or why you can't volunteer as a judge for the dog show. Yes, you can make up stories all right. Ideas are not exactly the same as excuses and lies, but all three can be intertwined in the creation of written fiction. This seems a long way from Anaïs Nin's noble statement, but it isn't really.

Inside every writer, inside every human being, there's a wealth of ideas and inspiration. New ideas are forever being added to the store, and the writer can go idea-shopping and decide which ones to buy. But how to decide? Some ideas insist on being used. So there's no problem in that case. But sometimes the writer has trouble choosing, and even imagines there are no ideas at all.

—*Writing Exercise*—
Maybe it helps to randomly pick a word for the day, and write around it freely and even carelessly. Some people meditate. Dreams can present material to you also. Listen to your dreams, because they might be messages for you. Why did I dream this or that? Stay with the dream, for while if you can, and you might have a flash of inspiration, if that's what you need. Of course, what you write and how you write and what you write about are all bound up together.

> *'Your own winning style must begin with ideas in your head.'*
> KURT VONNEGUT

—*Writing Exercise*—
When helping my students to find a direction for their thoughts, I suggest they concentrate on one image, and write from the focus of that image. In observing the way students work I have noticed that everyone has important, personal, key stories about certain things such as trees, houses, water. Somewhere in your memory is a story about a tree. If you start to write your tree story you will have no shortage of

ideas. If you write freely and courageously, this tree story will seem to write itself. Write something about water and something else about a house. You may be going back to your vivid memories of childhood. I have talked about this before.

'There is always one moment in childhood when the door opens and lets the future in.'
GRAHAM GREENE

—*Writing Exercise*—

Here is a program of exercises for you to follow in the process of exploring your ideas. It sounds too simple to be true, but give it a go. Write about three hundred words on each of the topics on the following list, writing on one topic a day. Begin with the words: 'I remember' and just go on freely from that. You will go beyond memory into other realms, but beginning with memory can be a good idea. There is something very satisfying about doing a small task such as this every day, feeling the progress as the days go by. You will also find that writing today's three hundred words has an effect on what you write tomorrow. Ideas feed on ideas, and writing skills build. They might look like baby steps, and maybe they are, but they kind of resemble five-finger exercises on the piano.

Topics

> Dark : Fire : Flower : Rock : Chair : River : School : Sun : Moon : Sky : Wedding : Funeral: Christmas : Apple : Toy : Hands : Mountain : Sea : Window : Music Teacher

When you have explored all these topics, others will suggest themselves to you. Some of them will grow longer, will develop into stories, finding a life of their own, a form of their own. I think one of the best books for you to read on this point is Nabokov's *Speak Memory*. It is nourishing and inspiring.

> *'In our childhood we know a lot about hands since they live and hover at the level of our stature: Mademoiselle's were unpleasant because of the froggy gloss on their tight skin besprinkled with ecchymotic spots.'*
> VLADIMIR NABOKOV

I think writers usually keep most of what they write, in notebooks or such, knowing that some of it will be useful and will one day be stories, but knowing also that much of it will never appear in a finished manuscript. So don't discard any of the work you do on the above topics.

Sometimes students can become quite inspired and productive if they are given an opening sentence from the story of another writer. They don't necessarily have to retain the sentence in their own work, but the quality of a good opening line is such that it may well lead to very good new writing.

Do the following sentences inspire you? They should inspire you to read the stories, but do they give you a feeling that you might be able to write like this?

> 'My cinder-grey room has a window, but I have never in all my time here looked out of it.'
> WILLIAM TREVOR, 'THE BLUE DRESS'

> 'All Olga's friends and acquaintances were at her wedding.'
> ANTON CHEKHOV, 'THE GRASSHOPPER'

> 'No living eye, of human being or caged wild beast or dear domestic animal, had beheld Mrs Lanier when she was not being wistful.'
> DOROTHY PARKER, 'THE CUSTARD HEART'

Notice the way all three take you straight into something very interesting, and promise more excitement. I love the way the Dorothy Parker one ends with that surprising 'wistful'. And I can't wait to get more detail about Olga's friends *and* acquaintances. Look at how powerful the adjective 'cinder-grey' is. This is an example of an adjective that is really working for the writer. First sentences like these get the writer and the reader off to a really good start. They have energy, the energy that comes from confidence and excitement about the project on the part of the writer. They *promise* something.

It isn't just that their subject matter sparks your interest, the construction of the sentences is also important. The length, the rhythm, the emphases.

I have given you a lot of hard work to do in answer to your question about inspiration, although inspiration is a word that suggests something spiritual. That is often the way with writing – you find that the practical matters and the spiritual matters seem to work together. In my next letter I will write some more about what you might call the spiritual side of writing.

> *'Go for a walk. It's inspirational. The body at work, the mind at rest – you can't beat that.'*
> CARRILLO MEAN

Before I go for my walk, I must say that writers get their ideas from their own heads, for heaven's sake. What they do with them is what matters, and becomes not just their own business, but the business of their readers. May your ideas and your readers be many.

With best wishes,

Virginia

Letter Twenty

THE EAR AND THE HEART

The Rhythms of Prose

'The sound of what falls on the page begins the process of testing it for truth.'
Eudora Welty

*D*ear Writer,
In the letters I have written to you I have usually tried to be practical and to avoid fanciful and airy-fairy ways of speaking about fiction writing. However, when I begin to speak about the rhythms of the prose, I know I will start to talk about magic. You see I believe that a mystery, a magic, inhabits the words themselves and is affected also by the way they are arranged. The writer is a magician who learns to work this magic. I know I sound completely loony, not to mention arrogant, when I say that. The writer must keep writing and writing until a true rhythm emerges in the sentences, until the sentences take a true shape. The shape they take will be the thought you are expressing. The rhythm is deep within the thought. If you read your sentences aloud you will learn to catch the tune, to know when the rhythm is true. The satisfactory sentence has the shape of the experience it describes, and also has the effect of shaping the reader's experience. You must trust your ear and your heart. This is

THE EAR AND THE HEART

no easy matter, but takes time and courage, vigilance and confidence. Confidence. When discussing with his students Kafka's *Metamorphosis*, Nabokov said:

> Curiously enough, Gregor the beetle never found out that he had wings under the hard covering of his back. This is a very nice observation on my part to be treasured all your lives. Some Gregors, some Joes and Janes, do not know that they have wings.

Perhaps you have wings.

You learn to trust your ear and your heart. Your sentence must lead the reader up to the meaning so that the meaning can dawn like light in the reader's mind. The ear, the heart, the brain, the stomach will work together if the sentence is right, for a good sentence is a human as well as a godly thing.

Your feeling for the rhythm of your prose can be awakened and nourished by reading different kinds of good fiction. Read aloud and savour the magic of the rhythm of the prose.

You can only discover how to work the magic by doing the writing. Always remember that what writers do is write. They might also sit on hilltops and gaze up at the stars (good), but unless they write some sentences, they are not writers. There are no short cuts, no matter what anybody tells you. The rhythm of the sentence comes gradually as you work towards finding it. When it is right, you will know that it is. You will find it and you will know that you have found it. Virginia Woolf wrote on this subject of the rhythm of the sentence:

> Style is a very simple matter; it is all rhythm. Once you get that, you can't use the wrong words. This is very profound, what rhythm is, and goes far deeper than words. A sight, an emotion, creates this wave in the mind, long

before it makes words to fit it, and in writing one has to recapture this, and set this working, (which has nothing apparently to do with words) and then, as it breaks and tumbles in the mind, it makes words to fit in.

Yay, Virginia!

The only way for you to find the rhythm of your own sentences is to write the sentences.

Wise Old Tale – The Happiest Man in the World
A man visited a sage and said, 'For years I have tried to be happy, but still I am always unsettled.' The sage replied, 'You must set out on a journey, seeking the happiest man in the world. When you find him, ask him for his shirt and put it on.'

The man met many happy men, but none was the happiest. At last, after many weary footsteps and many terrible adventures with bears and raging rivers and boiling sunlight, the traveller came to a wood where he heard the sound of laughter. He entered the wood and found a man whose face was hidden in shadow.

'Are you the happiest man in the world?' he asked.

'I am.'

'Then I have been instructed to ask for your shirt. Please will you give it to me?'

'Look closely at me, my friend,' said the happiest man. 'For I do not have a shirt.'

'What am I to do?'

> 'Listen and learn. Your search has given you what you need – the knowledge that happiness is not to be borrowed.'
>
> Then the traveller saw the face of the happiest man and it was the face of the sage who had sent him on his journey.
>
> 'Why did you not tell me this and save me a lot of trouble?'
>
> 'You needed to discover the truth for yourself. The quest with all its tribulations and sorrows was the necessary part.'

You can only discover how to work the magic by doing the writing. Right? You have to practise; you have to get the beat. Yes, you do. Please read aloud what you write, and keep reading aloud the wonderful things that other writers have written for you. As you gaze up at the stars, maybe you could shout your favourite sentence of the day. Just you and the night and the music. It could be a sentence by James Joyce, or perhaps it could be one by you. Imagine that.
Best wishes,

Virginia

Letter Twenty-One

WHEN ALL'S SAID AND DONE

The Final Draft

'There are three rules for writing a novel.
Unfortunately, no-one knows what they are.'
SOMERSET MAUGHAM

*D*ear Writer,
I was delighted to get the final draft of 'The Teeth' in the post today. In your accompanying letter you said you have done five complete rewrites of this story, and that you now know you have told the story you wanted to tell. The work you have done has been slow and painstaking, but the story has finally blossomed into life. You have gradually realised that your true interest was in seeing the busybody come to grief. The reader can feel the authority of your creation, as I am sure you felt the power of your authority when you typed the final draft.

(**Author's Note 2013**: Oh poor old Writer. All that typing, all those sheets of paper. How very smooth and swift and elegant things are now on my Mac. And now she gets to put it in the mail with a stamped self-addressed envelope and so forth. Those were the days.)

You may like to compare your first draft with your final one. In the process of rewriting, you have developed several useful techniques. You have acquired a firmer, different point of view, changing from the third to the first person. You have lost your timid tone and have acquired a ring of authority. You have removed nearly all the adverbs and many of the adjectives. You have not named the emotions but have shown the behaviour associated with them. You have removed much of the useless dialogue, and what remains is smooth and convincing. You have sketched the characters by using telling details. (I particularly like the part where the woman 'put out a small hand in a yellow kid glove' to shake the hand of the headmaster. Three adjectives, but they are all working for you. Shades of my ghostly imagining of Emma Bovary's ungloved hand.) You have created a world into which the reader has been transported.

You say in your letter that sometimes the words just seemed to flow and then fall into place. The reader can feel the effect of such magic and inspiration. When you write with authority the reader feels safe in going along with you. You have made the reader welcome. C.S. Lewis says that 'writing is like driving sheep down a road. If there is any gate to left or right, the readers will most certainly go into it.' So you need, maybe, to take your reader's hand.

You have succeeded in keeping the reader on the right path. You have obeyed the rules of style as set down by Conrad and Madox Ford. 'The Teeth' is now ready to be submitted to an editor or entered for a competition.

I wish you well with it. Do let me know how it goes.

This process you have gone through with exercises and rewrites of 'The Teeth' has in itself been an exercise. I think that in future you will probably find you write more freely and easily, will be able to apply the techniques you have used in a less conscious way, more instinctively. This will be very pleasurable, even at times ecstatic.

Very best wishes for the future,

Virginia O'Day

(***Author's Note 2013***: So those were the letters, Reader. You realise they represent pieces of paper flying around in envelopes, post offices, postmen, letter boxes. If Writer ever becomes famous she might sell them to a library. How about the formality of it all? If they were emails Virginia would just be saying Hi, or Hi Writer. Would she ever get her own name, I wonder. Well, next there are some pieces I am addressing to you. So read on.)

Story One and Analysis

'THE COMPANY OF LAUGHING SINGING INVISIBLES'

A SHORT STORY

Dear Writer is a piece of fiction about fiction. The following essay was written in 1997, and in 1998 I put up my own website www.carmelbird.com. So the essay is still a long way behind the writer's world of 2013. But as with the letters to Writer, the essay reveals aspects of writing fiction that might hold good for all time. It is a personal essay, a memoir of a kind.

I was writing the letters at the same time as I was writing a novel, *The Bluebird Café*, and the character of Virginia turned up in the novel. I found that she had been a teenage anorexic in the fifties, among other things. She now lives in Cambridge, Massachusetts, writing plays and novels, visiting Australia from time to time. I lead a quiet life in a Melbourne suburb, tapping away at my computer in front of a window that looks out onto a wall of bougainvillea which, as I write this, is ablaze with a colour I know only as American Beauty. The curtains – printed with images of the Unicorn Tapestries – are always drawn back to let in the light and the sight of the leaves and flowers outside.

Why I write fiction is a question that never really bothers me, but it is one that is so often asked, in one way or another, of writers, that I propose to explore the subject. It is one of the questions that lurks beneath the surface of the letters to Writer, but it is not one that Virginia or Writer ever ask each other. Lots of little children write down stories, but most people stop doing this when they grow up. Could it be that fiction writers are not quite grown up? I suppose it could. I do happen to believe that writing is helped if the writer can look at life and so forth with some of the freshness of a child's vision. That makes sense. Writers do have to notice things all the time.

I can trace my own attitude to fiction writing back into my early life, and this is partly what I am going to look at in this essay. I recall that when I was a teenager I used to write novels in notebooks, sometimes sitting in place called the Scotch Cemetery. It was a forlorn and creepy place where there were tombs cut into the hillside and sealed off with rusty iron doors. When I was seventeen I asked my mother to buy me a typewriter and she did, and I started to teach myself to type from a Pitman's manual. This was during the holidays from university – I would work in an ice-cream factory during the day, then at a café at night, and then I would do my typing practice. But it is one thing to say I knew I had to learn to type; it is another to know why I went to the trouble. I was driven by the belief that I would write fiction. And I wrote and I typed – until I had a story accepted (it was, as it happened, the first story I ever submitted for publication) by the *Australian Women's Weekly* in 1963. I knew nothing about small literary magazines then, although they did exist.

I was writing novels and destroying them – they were no good at all – I didn't need to be told. I was writing stories,

'THE COMPANY OF LAUGHING SINGING INVISIBLES'

steadily, quietly, and teaching in a high school. Then in the mid-seventies – I had pieces of short fiction published in the *Melbourne Herald Sun*. Some of them won prizes. Progress was still slow. I continue to write fiction. But why?

Consider this:

Once when I was five, my mother and my aunt and I came home from an afternoon at the cinema and we saw at once that the tapestry cushion had gone from the chair on the front veranda.

Long afterwards I discovered the cushion in the playhouse belonging to Mrs Hopper's daughter.

We were not supposed to have anything to do with Mrs Hopper because she was known to be 'not all there'. She lived across the street, and sometimes you would see her at the window – a small, thin woman with wild black hair. Her children were in boarding school; her husband was a wealthy pastrycook, the owner of a chain of cake shops. The Hoppers' house resembled a big white cake. It was in fact a Tasmanian version of Spanish Mission. I suppose Mrs Hopper had nothing much to do.

I have sometimes thought about Mrs Hopper, and I have realised that she was probably suffering from depression. I have a memory of one exciting incident – Mr Hopper was attacked in the driveway of their house by a rival pastrycook with a knife. There were police and cars in the street that day, and we didn't often get that. Mr Hopper wasn't killed, but he became the subject of more local interest and speculation than he had been before. He was a fat man in a navy suit.

This is not a straightforward story about my childhood, and it isn't a story about Mrs Hopper – it's a reflection on the possible origins of the images that have so lodged in my imagination as to require treatment in fiction, and on the possible reasons for my attitude to events both now and then. It is also a reflection on depression, on what it is that keeps people such as Mrs Hopper behind their curtains.

When I was in my twenties I read *The Feminine Mystique*. I realised that as a child I had been living in the midst of 'Housewife Syndrome' and that I had been silently documenting it for a long time. I remembered (well, I had never forgotten) that a woman who lived two houses away from Mrs Hopper drank a bottle of disinfectant and died. I wrote a story, 'Pomona Avenue', inspired by the dead woman who was the most dramatic and tragic of all the depressed women I had known in my childhood in rural Tasmania.

The awareness I had of the dark trouble that infected the lives of the women around me when I was very young has never left me, and it is sometimes at the back of my mind as I write. Men didn't suffer from this thing, as far as I could tell. This is not to say that men don't get depressed; but the men I knew when I was a child seemed to have more freedom to express themselves than the women had. They went out to work in the daytime during the week, and at night they read and wrote and worked in their sheds and workshops. On weekends they drove the car for family outings, or they went to the pub, the races, the football or the cricket, or they worked in the garden. They went to clubs and meetings. They were forever Meeting People and Doing Things. If it sounds pretty dull, I suppose it was. They did sometimes have recourse to doing such things as knifing each other in the driveway in broad daylight.

Behind the walls that shone white like icing, beyond the pathway that was lined with standard roses blooming pink and apricot in summer, Mrs Hopper existed alone with her depression. Her husband provided her with a little Spanish

'THE COMPANY OF LAUGHING SINGING INVISIBLES'

Mission palace, but it seemed he could not dissolve her sadness, supposing he wanted to. I have no idea. The house was to her a kind of prison; the lace and satin curtains were the window bars. She wandered through the rooms, doing nothing, pulling back the curtains to stare blankly into the street. Hoping to catch on to some strand of life as it blew past, hoping to see something shining or twirling, hoping to interrupt the dread grey flow of things, to intercept a message from the clouds, a code beamed in from a reality far, far away.

I never saw Mrs Hopper go out, but then, to tell the truth, I had more interesting things to think about. I paid very little attention to Mrs Hopper, not all there, across the street, behind her window. But I learnt, one day, that *she was watching us.*

My mother and aunt, living next-door to each other, had each other for company. I realise now how lucky they were. Supposing Mrs Hopper's sister had lived next-door to her, would that have helped? Maybe? If my mother and aunt had elements of Mrs Hopper's depression in their natures, they somehow kept the depression at bay, and never gave in the way Mrs Hopper did. They got their housework done and then they got out and about, played tennis and badminton. They cooked and cleaned and knitted and sewed and gardened. They read books and magazines. They sang. They *laughed*. They had card days and afternoon teas. Why wasn't Mrs Hopper ever included? Perhaps she was invited but never came. Shopping was a big thing; so was going to the cinema. Because I was the youngest child, when all the others had gone to school, I accompanied my mother and my aunt when they went to the pictures. I was like a kind of extra handbag they dragged along, and they made no concession to my taste in movies. I got lollies and ice-creams and was taken to the lavatory, but otherwise I was pretty nonexistent. I saw a lot of war films, the sky busy with aircraft and bombs, the sailors and soldiers and airmen on the screen large and handsome and black and white.

I was always silently impatient for the men to get whatever it was they had to do over and done with so that the pretty heroine could appear and there could be sweeter music and kissing and staring into each other's eyes. I liked the sex. It was tame enough, but I was thrilled by it, couldn't wait for the plot to get around to it. There was never enough. Sometimes there were films with no women at all, and no sex I could detect, and I was very disappointed. I didn't know anything about sex, you understand, but I knew a frisson when I felt one.

In some ways I was conscious that what kept Mrs Hopper prisoner in her house, prisoner in her own skin, was fear and a poor sex life. I realise I can enunciate that now with hindsight, but I believe that as a child I recognised it at some level for what it was.

On our front veranda, among the wicker furniture, there was a leather armchair, set well back, protected from the weather. In the armchair was a lovely fat cushion, one side of which was the tapestry picture of a woman in a frilly dress on a swing. The picture was a rendering of *The Swing* by Jean-Honoré Fragonard. Kitsch was the order of the day. We used to sit in the armchair and read or play or tell stories; and it was nice to stand on the cushion because it was soft and squashy underfoot. And I would take the cushion in my arms and sit on the bare leather chair, and I would trace the elements of the picture with my finger. The long ropes of the swing emerge from the trees as if from clouds. It's like

'THE COMPANY OF LAUGHING SINGING INVISIBLES'

something in a ballet – the elaborate, romantic dress of the woman is like a ballgown as it puffs out in the air. She tilts her head, smiling in a tantalising way, and her bonnet flips up at an angle. You can see the top of one of her stockings as, with the other foot, she kicks off her shoe. Lying on the ground, among the flowers beneath her is a man in silk and satin and lace, waving his hat at the woman, and gazing up her dress as it flies open. Strangely enough, in the shadows behind the swing, there is another man who is guiding the swing with another set of ropes. Stone cherubs on a particularly ugly dolphin look up at the woman, and a thoughtful naked person, man or woman, looks down on her from a pedestal.

So there I was, at the age of five, sitting on the veranda, fondling the shoe, running my finger up and down the ropes, feeling the treetops with the flat of my hand, always coming back to the man in the shadows who was pulling the strings, and always staring into the nasty open mouth of the dolphin.

Years later when I saw the original of *The Swing* in the Wallace Collection, the picture was much brighter and lighter than the old tapestry cushion, but I couldn't get rid of my childhood feeling that the woman was in danger, that the moment was somehow fatal, that the naked foot revealed by the flying shoe was vulnerable, that the man with the hat was tricking the woman on the swing, that the man in the shadows was powerful and evil, that the cherubs were fearful for the woman, that the dolphin was malign. I used to stare and stare at that picture on the cushion. One man controlling a woman on a swing so that another man can see up her dress.

The man on the ground is a portrait of the Baron de Saint-Julien who commissioned the painting; the woman is a portrait of his mistress (nameless?); the man in the shadows is a portrait of an unnamed bishop. That's all I know about it, but I tell you, when I was little I thought it was pretty funny stuff.

Once when I was a child at the beach I wanted to have a go on the metal slide. The only people around were me and two boys I didn't know. The boys took no notice of me until I reached the top of the ladder ready to go down. Then one boy sprang to the top of the ladder and the other one stood at the bottom of the slide. As soon as I set off, the one at the top dropped a beer bottle onto the slide, and the one at the bottom threw a stone at it and so I was sliding with bare legs on broken glass. They ran away.

There is a connection there with what I feel about *The Swing*. Dark times in rural Tasmania.

The cushion was one of the many ways into fantasy. But not far away, across the street and down the hill there were women seeking fantasy, women trapped, to one degree or another, in boredom, in frustration, losing sight of their realities, dropping out of view behind the curtains, below the level of the black waters of depression, into the jaws of the lurking dolphin. They would kill themselves, on rare occasions, out of the blue, with poison, or by jumping off the King's Bridge. Mrs Hopper didn't do anything; she drifted around the house, growing paler, becoming translucent, like some underwater creature becoming invisible among the floating weeds. Mrs Hopper, they said in serious, low tones, suffers from melancholia. I voiced this once, and my mother told me I should never say that word.

One day, when my mother and aunt and I came home from the pictures, we saw that the tapestry cushion had gone from the chair on the veranda. It was nowhere to be found.

'THE COMPANY OF LAUGHING SINGING INVISIBLES'

This was a moment of powerful realisation and sensation for me. I have never really learnt to acknowledge the disappearance of things; I still always go round and round in desperate circles searching for the thing that has gone, imagining it back in its place. My mother would pray to Saint Anthony; I pray to Saint Anthony. Often this works; but in the case of the tapestry cushion, the prayer was a long time in being answered.

But for ages the disappearance was a complete mystery. Eventually the cushion was replaced by one on which there was a scene displaying hunting dogs. It lacked the power of the woman on the swing.

A few years later, when she was about eight, Mrs Hopper's daughter Marion came home from boarding school on vacation. She was allowed to have a birthday party arranged by one of her aunts. I was invited. There was a dress code for parties: a girl had to have black patent shoes with ankle straps, silky white socks, and a dress made from organdie. My dress was dreamy pink with black velvet bows, inspired by something Deanna Durbin was wearing in a framed, signed portrait that hung beside my sister's bed. We also had, from my mother's childhood, a signed photograph of Mary Pickford. I remember the sight of all the organdie dresses at the party, dresses like flowers in a garden, pale poppies floating, roses opening in the sun. All hair was curled, all faces shining.

Mr Hopper took some photos as we sat around a table on the back lawn, under a willow tree. There was fairy bread with hundreds and thousands, butterfly cakes, chocolate frogs in green jelly set into the top of a sponge cake. Remember Mr Hopper was a pastrycook. The birthday cake itself was a fruit cake decorated with white icing all roughed up and studded with pink rosebuds in which stood eight candles. As well as the candles there were fine miniature silk flags. Union Jacks and Australian flags which we always had on our birthday cakes. The flags had to be removed before you lit the candles for fear the silk would catch fire.

Mrs Hopper stood wanly about in a navy blue dress with a very old-fashioned white lace collar. Her hair was done neatly in a bun; she fascinated me. She stood in the doorway, a picture of bewildered melancholy, a stick-figure waiting for the party to be over.

Happy Birth-day, dear Mar-ion.

We played Pin the Tail on the Donkey, and had a treasure hunt, following clues and finding bracelets and rings in cunning places. Then some of us went into Marion's playhouse where all the furniture was small and made from plywood and cane. Everything there was miniature and flimsy. Except for one thing – the tapestry cushion with the picture of the woman on the swing.

I knew it was our cushion; and I still know it was ours. But I said nothing. It was as if I had been caught in a misdemeanour, the transgression of knowing. I was in possession of a piece of secret truth. I was thrilled. I had the power to tell or not to tell. I decided it was more interesting not to tell. There was innocent Marion in her pale lemon dress with gorgeous apricot flounces, bustling about her playhouse, unaware of the several meanings attached to the cushion. She was fat like her father. It is of course possible that the Hoppers had an identical cushion, which had been discarded and abandoned in the playhouse; but I didn't think so. I was quite sure it was ours.

In an instant the scene came to me.

'THE COMPANY OF LAUGHING SINGING INVISIBLES'

My mother and aunt and I are out at the pictures. We are in the dark, the three of us, sitting on the red plush seats, watching the flickering screen. We are all warm and close; I am leaning against my mother, a paper bag of pink and white toffee and coconut in my hands. A dashing man in evening dress embraces a woman in a gown like a satin nightdress. They are on a terrace in the moonlight. The next day, the man will go to war.

Mrs Hopper, wearing a sad, dark flowery dress that is too big for her, too long and much too wide, saw us leave the house in a flurry of hats and gloves and handbags. Such drama and excitement. She saw us going down the hill, imagined us catching the tram, arriving at the pictures and getting the tickets, going in, sitting down. The red velvet seats. It gets dark. Can she even begin to imagine the paper bag of pink and white sticky lollies?

In her stockinged feet she patters down her front path, hesitates at the gate, and then keeps going. She crosses the sleepy road and opens our gate, brushes past the cypress hedge, pads up the path between the rose bushes, past the palm tree, up the steps onto the veranda. She pauses, looks back at her house, almost loses her nerve. Then she sits down in the armchair, sighs, leans back and shuts her eyes. It's not the first time she has done this; a couple of times before she has spent the afternoon on our veranda when we were out. This is the great adventure, getting out, crossing over, trespassing, stealing the air on our veranda.

Time passes.

Unable to see her own house because our hedge is in the way, she begins to imagine it, shuts her eyes and thinks of her empty house staring at her from across the street. Imagines one day going further, stepping off our veranda and tiptoeing down the hill, around the bend, over the next hill – and away. If she went, they would find her and bring her back. She has sometimes heard of people who disappear, who go out to buy a newspaper or a pound of butter or a bag of onions and are never seen again. The daring, the planning. And an instinct in her tells her she belongs to those people. How to get to them? Where is that company of laughing, singing invisibles? Gathered round the tables in a distant inn, they tell each other stories of far away and long ago when they were shop assistants and postmen and barristers-at-law and the wives of prominent pastrycooks. Another life, they say. That was me, they say, in another life.

Mrs Hopper opens her eyes and sees that the shadows on the grass are lengthening. Must be getting home. Must make a move, cross the road, cross the river, bridge the gap. She can scarcely bear to get out of the armchair. She stands up, takes a breath, and makes as if to leave. Then on the spur of the moment, in the twinkling of an eye, she turns around and scoops up the tapestry cushion, holds it close, hugs it, buries her face in it and weeps. Swiftly the tears bubble from her eyes, pour in terrible droplets onto the woman on the swing. Teardrops stain the dress, the blossoms on the trees; the hands of the bishop are slippery with salty tears. The dolphin opens wide his grinning jaws and drinks the teardrops in. The Baron de Saint-Julien takes his hat and with it wipes from his eyes the billowing tears of the sorrowful Mrs Hopper.

She burrows her face in the cushion for one despairing moment and then, the cushion in her arms, she dashes from our garden, across the road, back into the safety of her own prison-house. She shuts her door and sinks down beside a marble pedestal on which rests the marble head of a

'THE COMPANY OF LAUGHING SINGING INVISIBLES'

girl wearing a marble bonnet. For a long time Mrs Hopper huddles at the foot of the pedestal, crying almost silently into the cushion.

In due course, somebody tosses the cushion, a foreign, unexplained damp object, into Marion's playhouse.

A woman comes each morning to do Mrs Hopper's housework, hoovering the flowery carpets, shaking the silky drapes, dusting the china ornaments, washing, ironing, straightening, putting the dinner on. One day the woman finds a strange, pictorial cushion – a man lying on the ground looking up a woman's dress.

Do you want this Mrs Hopper? Oh, no, Iris, just put it in the garden shed or something.

Too pretty, in a way, for the shed, it goes into the playhouse. The wily hand of St Anthony of Padua places it in Marion's playhouse where it waits in patient silence, woman on swing caught in laughing motion, waits until I come to have my prayers answered, and silently identify my property.

And just as I somehow understood that one thing Mrs Hopper needed was a decent sort of sex life – falling into the keen embrace of Errol Flynn perhaps? – I also understood her romance with the cushion. The cushion was a trophy, a piece of booty from our veranda. It was a comfort, a triumph – and finally an embarrassment, a hollow victory. But what on earth do you do with a thing like that, once you have stolen it and taken it home? If she gave it to Iris, who knows, it could end up where it came from. The ways of housekeepers with strange stolen cushions are devious and dark. Not easy to conceal, the cushion goes, oversized, on a chair in Marion's playhouse.

My discovery, the answer to my prayer, made the party brighter and more interesting for me. Forget the frog-pond cake, the fluttering butterfly cakes with cream and jelly, the rose-embossed birthday cake – I had a piece of awful knowledge.

Awful knowledge. Mrs Hopper was a *thief*. Now that was the kind of thing I collected.

And thoughts are easier to hide than cushions. The whole business was filed in my memory. I went about my own affairs calmly, piecing together stuff to feed my understanding of how the world around me worked. I kept notebooks in which I drew pictures of hundreds and hundreds of families, all the members named and given biographies. The intricacies of their stories and relationships absorbed me – such talents, such deformities. I could dish out to these people anything I liked. The notebooks were for me alone. They were ways into thrilling secretive worlds to which only I had access. If you asked me what I was doing, so busy with my notebook, I would tell you I was doing nothing. But I filled a pile of large Spirax books that my father used to give me.

I drew a picture of the interior of Marion's playhouse, and I put the cushion, sketched in great detail, on a chair.

The episode of the knifing by the rival pastrycook had gone into a story long before – a matter of marital infidelity, of which there was quite a bit about the place – and also the embezzlement of funds.

Because I now write fiction professionally, people sometimes ask me how long I have been writing, and when it was I first decided to become a writer, and where I get my ideas from. I was at it long before the episode with the Fragonard cushion – but it was incidents such as this that nourished and confirmed me in what I do.

I think it's a bit odd the way so many people quiz writers about how long, why. I sense that painters, for instance, are

'THE COMPANY OF LAUGHING SINGING INVISIBLES'

not so often asked these questions. I daresay it is so because the fabric of fiction is the stuff of everyday life, and the words are free, and the materials for writing are pretty cheap too. So the questions people ask writers are partly about why the writer can write, or imagines she can, while so many other people with, it would appear, similar material, cannot, or at least do not, do it.

In my own case, perhaps part of the answer lies in my position as the youngest girl, adrift from my sisters while they went to school, alone with women who were busy with their own imaginations, telling each other stories of their lives and observations. The things I heard during afternoon teas would make your hair curl. Nobody thought I was listening, let alone understanding. Sometimes someone would say that little pigs have big ears, but then they would laugh and continue anyway. As if little pigs were not going to stash the stuff away and reproduce it fifty years down the track. I listened and made the best of the materials I was given. And the thing, the process, got a grip on me early – never mind that I was forty-six before I had a novel published by a real publisher. It was an obsession; it still is an obsession. I can't tell you the fun I have had writing this essay. Part of the answer to the question of why I write fiction is in here somewhere. Perhaps if I ever find the old Spirax cartridge notebooks I might get some more clues. But only clues.

I write fiction because I believe it is the thing I do best.

Mrs Hopper died of old age.

Her name was not Mrs Hopper.

Story Two and Analysis

THE WRITING MECHANISM AND WRITING TO ORDER

I am writing this essay on April 23, 2013. In April 1993 I had a meeting with the editor of my collection of stories *The Common Rat*. The editor said the book was one story short. I said I didn't have another story to add. She said: 'You are a writer. Write one.' So I did. I wish I could tell you which story it was that I wrote, but I can't remember; I keep erratic and eccentric notebooks, and some of them are in the National Library so I can't easily check them. But somewhere in the collection is a story that was written to order. The editor had reminded me of my business, and her words often come back to me. Her name is Meredith Rose; thank you, Meredith.

Before writing that collection, I had been interested in the role of rats in human affairs, and since the publication I have continued to collect notes and news cuttings about rats. By a coincidence there is today a news story from the nuclear plant at Fukushima. I quote from *The New York Times*:

> A blackout disabled cooling at four fuel pools last month, an event the company traced to a

> rat that might have gnawed on power cables and caused a short circuit. Engineers found its scorched body in a damaged switchboard.

They had found 'the charred body of a rat' that had chewed through the electric cables. I often think of the epigraph to *The Common Rat:* Wherever there is a good habitat for a rat, there a rat will be.

The rat continues to find a habitat in my imagination, not necessarily in my fiction. But my fiction is so bound up in my day-to-day life that it is almost impossible to tease out the elements of the two.

Time and again aspiring writers ask practising writers about the sources of their ideas, and about how those sources translate into fiction. It is one of the key questions in the quester's quest for the secret to writing stories. Time and again the practising writer will try to explain that there is no secret formula, but the quester comes back again like the fat man looking for the secret pill that will trim his body down. There is *no secret*, there is *no pill*. A little phrase from parents and teachers past echoes in my mind like a refrain: 'How many times do I have to tell you?' If you write stories, you write stories – that is what you do. Get on with it.

So anyway, Meredith reminded me that my business is to write stories, and ever after when someone has asked me to write a story for some reason or other, I have written one. Oh, the *pleasure* in being able to do that. Recently someone asked for a story with a supernatural element to it. I had only ever written one such story before, also in response to a request, but I had a very good time constructing the new story. Even more recently I was invited to contribute a story to the online *Review of Australian Fiction*. There was no prescription as to genre or style or subject matter – just 'a short story'. So my imagination (or whatever it is that goes to work) was on the alert – I was in the process of what is called 'writing a story'. This moment is probably the one that bothers new writers the most. If they don't know what they are supposed to be writing *about*, how can they choose, and decide, what it is they will do? In my own case, at this point, life puts in my path the elements, the materials if you like, and my writing mechanism goes to work. I only just now invented that term 'writing mechanism', but I like it, and I have decided to use it as the title for this essay.

Just a note here about the subject matter of short stories. I think generally that the big topics are human nature and human relationships. Is that right? But after that the field is wide open. Once I wrote a story that focused on the idea of aunts, and a critic said that this was not a good idea because aunts are not interesting. Well, not interesting to that critic, I suppose, but how could she presume to pronounce for everyone. Did she mean the *writing* was not interesting? Why not say so? It is a mistake critics often make – they fail to address what the writer is doing (or trying to do), and are either lazy, or else blinded by their own response to the subject matter. It would be good if they could bring themselves to say that the subject matter is boring or troubling to them personally, and then get on with reading the work. Of course, it is perhaps difficult to separate the subject from the ways the writer has dealt with it, but that could be one of the challenges of being a critic.

Fiction is storytelling; storytelling consists of the story and the telling. When the story *and* the telling work together, then the magic is made. Let's get back to the story I wrote for the *Review of Australian Fiction*. I will let you read the story, and then I'll examine some of its writing mechanism.

'FROM PARADISE TO WONDERLAND'

A SHORT STORY

I drove past the house yesterday. It's twenty-three years now, twenty-three years since we all left. Well, we left in stages, bit by bit, but it's certainly twenty-three years since I loaded the old Pajero and the camping trailer and headed off. Packed up to the gills. The kids, the dog and the kitchen sink. I can't believe I did it, now that I think back. We ended up in Byron, but we started out, at the house in beautiful Tasmania, with grape vines like a green pattern on a blanket sloping away down the hillside.

We left the dog with my sister Emily in Burnie. That was just about my one regret. Jake and Skye were heartbroken. They had had Loopy all their lives, but I promised them they could have any pet they wanted when we got where we were going. Where are we going then, they said. And I said we were going to Wonderland. It just came out, and as soon as I had said it I was sorry. What a dumb thing to say, but I was desperate I suppose. Skye said the only pet she wanted anyway was Loopy, and she whimpered and blubbered off and on for six days and nearly drove me out of my mind.

I wanted Loopy too, but there was no way. Try listening to 'Loooooopy' day in day out in the back of the car, not to mention on the ferry and in every McDonald's and KFC along the highway. But as I say, it only lasted for six days, and then she seemed to get over it. Jake was mostly silent, thank God, but I know he was mourning for Loopy – well, for a lot of things.

People sometimes say that the destination is not as important as the journey. Well I am here to tell you that sometimes it's the destination that matters, and you can stick the journey up your jumper. Let's just say it was hell and leave it at that. These days the kids remember it fondly, the junk food, the fly-blown motels, the caravan parks, the wind-blown playgrounds full of plastic bags and broken bottles. People were kind. I will say that. Although there was the boy that stole Jake's scooter. The hardest thing, actually, was keeping our clothes clean. I was forever seeking out laundromats and trying to collect enough coins. And everything came out grey anyway. Mum, Skye would say, mum, when do we get to Wonderland? It's a long way, I would say, a long way. But we'll get there in the end, baby. And we did.

My friend Gretel was living in Byron with her man of the time. That was Snoddy. She was making bead jewellery and selling it in markets, and Snods was doing huge paintings – mainly tropical flowers – frangipani and hibiscus and so on. They were popular at the time with big banks and hotels in the cities, they were hung on vast marble walls. He used to sing 'I dreamt I dwelt in marble halls.' I still see the paintings sometimes, in the odd bank and so forth. I always thought they were hideous, and I still do, but they certainly paid the bills. So we settled down with Gretel and Snoddy and their kids. Jake and Skye fitted right in, and I got a job in

'FROM PARADISE TO WONDERLAND'

a wine bar, cleaning and also serving drinks. This is the life, eh Tabbycat, Snoddy would say to me. Aren't you glad you made the effort? And I was. I put the terrible journey north – it went on forever – behind me, and got into the swing of things in Byron. I got into crystals and Tarot easy as, and into a bit of massage. Snoddy built me a wigwam and I operated from there. One day Skye said to me – I remember this as if it was yesterday – she said, Wonderland is wonderful, Mum. You were right to come here. I love it. And then she hugged me and she said, I love you forever, Mum. We wore flowers in our hair, and the atmosphere was sweet with patchouli and cannabis. The kids went to school in bare feet. They took to it all like ducks to water. Jake learnt to play the bongos, and Skye began the dancing that finally took her to New York. So this was Wonderland.

As I drove by the house on the hill yesterday, it was hard to believe I had done what I had done, broken from my life there at the vineyard. Escaped. I can go over it all in my mind now without really feeling the horror and the fear – horror and chaos every day, fear of the future. The legal battles were to come, as I drove off with the kids from that failed Paradise on the hill.

I suppose it all started when I fell in love with Salv. Yes. And we had a double wedding with his brother Fabio. Wedding bells like that should ring alarm bells, in retrospect. The brothers bought the vineyard and started to build the house on the hill – the famous double house where two families would live together with one fabulous swimming pool and stables for horses – and a vast garage splitting the house in two. That word 'splitting'. Always watch out for splitting.

Fabio married Anka – Anka with the shining golden hair and wide dreaming aquamarine eyes. She was the great beauty of the district. We were a lovely mixture of Italian, Anglo and Polish. It *was* a lovely mixture, truly, but in the end it didn't work. Watch out for 'mixture' too. That's another word. Mixture and splitting and alarm bells. Anka's family were holocaust survivors – her mother was one of the babies smuggled out of Poland in a big leather handbag. I thought her married name – Anka Foglieri – was really pretty, whereas mine – Tabitha Foglieri – was kind of a mouthful. Mixture. My mother – as Anglo as they come, and they came pretty Anglo in Tassie in the sixties – believed that the world should somehow resemble the world of Beatrix Potter, and yes, I was named after Tabitha Twitchit, the mother cat in the apron. Everybody used to give me figurines of her – I faithfully collected them for years. In fact I hated them. When I left the vineyard, they stayed behind in the shadow box on the wall of Skye's bedroom. I have sometimes wondered what became of them. They might be worth a fortune now. Too bad.

Things went well for a few years. We were the envy of the district with a flourishing vineyard and wine label 'Tabianka Cellars', and our great mansion on the hill. The Foglieri Castle – that's what people called it, the Foglieri Castle. Foglieri Folly more like.

I don't know when the rows started, but the rot set in, and while the vines flourished, the lives of the two families in the castle started to go to hell. Gretel said she saw it coming long before I did – well she had her crystal ball up there in Byron. Salv fell in love with Anka, didn't he. I think, to her credit, that she resisted him for a long time, but in the end Fabio caught them in the cabana and went after Salvatore with a shotgun. He never explained why he was carrying the gun at the time. Anyhow, he only threatened, didn't pull the trigger, but it was going to be only a matter of time. The stress of it all actually killed my mother. We tried to sort things out – counsellors and priests and lawyers, not to mention the families and friends, but it went from bad to worse and in the end I packed the Pajero and got out. I hardly even planned it. The big casualty at that point was Loopy, but actually he lived a long and happy life with Emily and Tom and their kids. We got another golden Lab before too long in Byron, and so everyone was happy. Well that sounds kind of neat. Nothing was neat, really, was it, not with everything simmering away at the Foglieri Folly. Simmering? More like doing whatever it is volcanoes do. Salvatore's dad came from Naples, and whenever he got into a temper the family used to call him Vesuvius. Well Vesuvius was about to blow.

While we were settling, or drifting down in Wonderland, there was trouble, naturally, back in Paradise. Big trouble. Fabio did eventually go after Salvatore with the shotgun. He killed him down among the vines very early one crisp morning in spring. 'Let us get up early to the vineyard' – that's from the Bible. Then he went up to the house and had a swim. He was still in the pool when the police came. So Fabio went to jail. Simple. Anka had a complete breakdown. It all worked out like an equation. I had to go back of course, but when it was all over, Salvatore's funeral and the trial, and so forth, I went back to Byron for good.

It seems strange to tell these terrible facts so bluntly, but they have kind of solidified in my mind, and I trot them out like an old legend or something. My children have no father any more. I have never really spoken to Anka since I left, all those years ago. Of course, we have had many legal dealings – we sold the house – and we see each other at funerals. I must say she looks very beautiful in black, with lace obscuring her face and her aquamarine eyes gazing sorrowfully out. I do feel sorry for her, yes, I do.

Some people from France, actually, bought the house and the business, and they didn't change the label because it has been so successful, particularly overseas. So there they are in grog shops all over the world, sparkling glass bottles with a picture of the house on the hill and the vines plaiting their way down the hillside in the sunlight, and the word 'Tabianka' scrawled in thick blue handwriting across the middle. Gretel laughs a kind of dark laugh and calls it one of the ironies of the gods. And more ironic is the fact that we can't usually afford to drink anything as expensive as Tabianka, even though we are doing well. Sometimes we do though. I thought it would choke me, but it is so smooth and rich that even I am completely seduced.

Snoddy eventually went off to live in Perth with a young woman who worked, as it happened, for a bank where they had one of his big flower paintings – it was a waterlily one – nothing like Monet. *He dreamt he dwelt in marble halls.* So that left Gretel and me and five kids. The kids have more or less gone now, and that leaves Gretel and me. We have a pretty good business providing massage and aromatherapy to all the big hotels from Byron and points north. My old wigwam is still there out the back.

Well, the drive past the house on the hill, with its sloping carpet of vines, brought it all back to me. It's all behind me now. Listen to your heart, Gretel used to say – she still does. I listened then and I listen now, and the answer is not difficult to hear. Of course, then you have to have the strength to follow it. That was the hard part – remember Loopy and the laundromats and the broken bottles in the playgrounds. But now there is Gretel and me, at home in Wonderland.

Whatever next, I say, whatever next, and Gretel smiles her enigmatic smile and holds me in her arms and says whatever will be will be. And I suppose it will.

Points on the Writing of the Story
One: A key element of the story is the house. Here is its origin: I live in the country, and was on the train to the city. This was when my writing mechanism was in the process of getting a story to send to the *Review of Australian Fiction*. The journey is familiar, and I always look out at one point along the way to gaze up across a vineyard to an impressive sprawling house on the top of a hill. People say that two brothers built this house, and lived in two parts of it with their families. The families, so goes the myth, quarrelled, and the house had to be sold.

Two: A small point that also came from the journey is the matter of how Anka's mother was supposedly smuggled out of Poland. The train stopped at a suburban station, and on the platform there was a billboard. It was an advertisement for a newspaper. The picture on the billboard was a huge photograph of Mirka Mora who is a beloved local painter. She was described on the billboard in type as a grandmother; she looked sweet and charming, and was holding a pretty china teacup. I know Mirka, and I can imagine the fun she must have had constructing that image. In the type alongside was information about Mirka, including the fact that she was a survivor of the holocaust of World War Two. I took a photo of the billboard on my phone. The woman in the seat opposite me saw me do this, and she said: 'Oh, I had an email about that woman just this morning. She used to smuggle babies out of Germany in her handbag. In the war. She was nominated for the Nobel Prize, but Al Gore got it.' Oh, the wonders of storytelling.

Three: Suddenly the house on the hill and the war in Europe came up against each other and the mechanism of the story started to tick away like a little clock. By the time I had been to the city and had boarded another train and got home that afternoon, I was ready to start writing.

Four: The voice of the narrator, Tabitha, spoke the first sentence, and the story was up and running. Now where does a writer get that narrator? That is one of the mysteries (sorry about that) of the process. She, the character, the narrator, leapt up, leapt out, and there she was, telling the story of the house. She was talking in 2013, and the story begins today, goes back twenty-three years so she can tell her story, and returns to 2013 at the end.

Five: Structure – I didn't know where it was going to end. All I knew was that she used to live in the house, left the house, and was telling the story. It was one of those cases where the storyteller of fiction seems to take over from the author of the whole thing. You hear writers say this happens. Some writers say it never happens. Some say it shouldn't happen. I just revel in the fact that it *does* happen. I don't write out plots – I just let the story take me along with it. There is a beautiful drive and energy. But it is my world, my history, my newspaper cuttings, my fellow travellers, my rats that find their way into the fabric of the story.

Six: In the period following World War Two, Australia welcomed people from countries such as Italy and Poland, and these people brought with them customs and traditions that have become part of life in Australia. The vineyard suggested Italians to me, and so the brothers were Italian.

And then I got into the idea of the mixture – the first generation of Anglo-Australians to marry the Europeans. And then there was the Polish girl. So the subject matter began to foreground the issue of migration and social change. I wouldn't say I set out to write a story *about* those things.

Seven: I have a friend who says she wishes life resembled the world of Beatrix Potter, and I think she is not alone in that. People often lean towards a comforting fairy tale and long to inhabit it. To their peril, I think. It always disturbs me when I hear my friend express that idea.

Eight: At this time I was also working as a contributing editor to the *Griffith Review* for their November 2013 issue, the topic of which is the fairy tale. So fairy tales are on my mind. The first fairy tale element that made its way into the story was the use of the name 'Gretel'. I didn't think about it – it just appeared. I left it there. It is always possible for a writer to change anything in the work, but Gretel seemed right. I had no idea at the time of Gretel's arrival in the narrative that she was in fact a key player. The word 'Wonderland' also came of its own accord, and obviously took the story (as well as Tabitha's journey) where it had to go.

Nine: Also at the same time as the writing of the story, the government of New Zealand passed legislation legalising same sex marriage. On the TV news I saw a placard in the crowd outside the court. It showed the image of the Disney Cinderella kissing the Disney Snow White. Those two famous profiles suddenly coming together lips to lips. And so there were Gretel and Tabitha in each other's arms at the end of the story. It turned out to be quite a journey for Tabitha. The movement from 'Paradise' to 'Wonderland' gave the story its shape and its structure.

Ten: It is always important to get the time frame right. Although there are no dates given in the story, the narrative is anchored in the war and migration details, and so I set out a timeline for myself, making sure the ages of all the characters – from the mother who named Tabitha, to the career of her grand-daughter Skye as a dancer in New York – were logical.

Eleven: The central drama of the story is the murder of one brother by the other. That is the event on which the story turns. Always human nature and human relationships. Reality seems to have killed off Tabitha's poor mother, by the way. Well, it was all shocking, wasn't it?

Twelve: I have said little about the actual *writing* of the story – the sentences, the paragraphs, the vocabulary, the rhythm. Those things come with practice.

Thirteen: And they lived happily ever after.

I think that's enough points. Writers often say they don't know what they are writing about, really, until they have finished. And one doesn't usually indulge in the flurry of analysis I have outlined here. I did it for *you*, Dear Reader, I did it for you.

It has occurred to me that one of the attractions the short story has for me both as a reader and a writer is the ability the form has to provide moments of illumination, to draw together delicate strands of emotion, character, incident, theme, subject – and to do something akin to what a conjurer does with coloured silk handkerchiefs, pulling them all in to make a ball, and then, with a flourish, opening them up as a brilliant full-blown rose.

Afterword

A NOTE ON QUOTATIONS IN THE TEXT

Many of the quotations included in the letters to 'Dear Writer' are quotations written hastily into my notebooks over many years. I did not always include the sources, although I was always sure to write the name of the author who said or wrote the words in the first place. Consequently, I have been unable to acknowledge the sources from which much of the quoted material in *Dear Writer Revisited* has come. I believe these quotations can be an inspiration and a comfort to other writers, and I thank the authors who wrote them.

Acknowledgements

Without you, the Reader, and without the help of Glenda Millard, Simon Groth, Bruce Carruthers, Susan Bassett and the publisher, Bronwyn Mehan, *Dear Writer Revisited* would not, Dear Reader, be in your hands today. I thank them, and I thank you also.

—Carmel Bird 2013
www.carmelbird.com

BOOKS BY CARMEL BIRD

NOVELS

Child of the Twilight — Cape Grimm
Red Shoes — The White Garden
The Bluebird Café — Crisis
Unholy Writ — Open For Inspection
Cherry Ripe

SHORT STORY COLLECTIONS

The Essential Bird
Automatic Teller
The Common Rat
The Woodpecker Toy Fact
Woodpecker Point
Births, Deaths and Marriages

ANTHOLOGIES

Home Truth
The Penguin Century of Australian Stories
The Stolen Children – Their Stories
Red Hot Notes
Daughters and Fathers
Relations – Australian Short Stories

WRITING MANUALS

Writing the Story of Your Life
Dear Writer
Not Now Jack – I'm Writing a Novel

CHILDREN'S BOOKS

The Fabulous Finola Fox
The Cassowary's Quiz
The Mouth

Index

A

Abstract noun 69
Adjective 8, 92, 108
Adler, Renata 80
Adverb 8
Adverb plus verb 10
Agents 98
Amis, Martin 71
Anderson, Jessica 96
Anderson, Sherwood 11
Arabian Nights, The 5
Atmosphere 8
Austen, Jane xvii, 61

B

Baby, manuscript and jewels 41
Bagnold, Enid 95
Banville, John 35
Block (writer's block) 31, 86, 87
Blog xvii, 83
Bloomsbury 99
Blyton, Enid 46
Borges, Jorge 53
Bradbury, Malcolm 83, 86
Bradbury, Ray 30
Brande, Dorothea 36, 82

C

Calvino, Italo 92
Capote, Truman 21, 29
Carey, Peter 3, 16, 34
Carroll, Lewis 50
Carter, Angela 2
Character 3
Chekov, Anton 85, 92, 107
Christie, Agatha 1, 4, 5, 53
Cinderella Complex, The 1
Clair, Daphne 91
Cliché 64, 65
Cocteau, Jean 85
Coincidence 43
Common sense 87
Conflict 40
Conrad, Joseph 56, 115
Courage 14, 18, 76, 88
Critics 134

D

Dialogue 65, 67
Dickens, Charles xvii, 38, 44, 61
Dowling, Colette 1
Drabble, Margaret 15
Dreams, recorded 80
Du Maurier, Daphne xx

E

East Anglia University 83
Eco, Umberto 52
Editing 13
Epstein, Joseph xvii
Estés, Clarissa Pinkola xxiii, 28
Exercises (writing) 4, 5, 11, 24, 32, 35, 39, 48, 50, 54, 60, 67, 105, 106

F

Fabric of fiction 131
Fabric of the story 142
Fantasy 124
Feminine Mystique, The 120
Festivals xviii, 82
Final draft 114
First person narrative 23
Fitzgerald, F. Scott 23, 30, 33, 44
Flaubert, Gustave 92
Ford, Ford Madox 56, 115
Foster Wallace, David 71
Fragonard, Jean-Honoré 122

G

Gadd, Lawrence 61
Galway, James xviii

Garner, Helen 16, 41
Gary, Romain 51
Gatsby, Jay 67
Greene, Graham 72

H

Hardy, Thomas 3
Harry Potter 62, 98
Hart, Josephine 47
Heaney, Seamus 37
Heelis, Frederick 73
Hemingway, Ernest 45, 73, 88
Heyer, Georgette 54
Hitler 55
Hodge, Jane Aitken 54
Humpty Dumpty 8

I

Ideas 104, 133
Imagination xx, 2, 7, 49, 133
Innes, Michael 18
Inspiration xxi, 104
Interior monologue 23
Iowa Writers' Workshop 82
Irony 70

J

James, Henry 79
Jargon 65
Job, other than writing 86
Jolley, Elizabeth 49
Journals, personal 77
Joyce, James 70, 96, 113

K

Kafka, Franz 111
King, Stephen xx, 5, 77
Koch, Christopher 17

L

Latinisms 68
Lavin, Mary 47
Lawrence, D.H. 100, 101
Le Carré, John xxiv, 86
Lewis, C.S. 115
Lists 31

M

McCullers, Carson 54
McDonald, Roger 24
McEwan, Ian 94 Magic 110
Magic formula xix
Malcolm, Janet 61
Mansfield, Katherine 21
Mantel, Hilary 71
Manuscript preparation 100
Márquez, Gabriel García 24, 43, 45, 51, 52
Maughham, Somerset 114
Mean, Carillo 27, 108
Mixed metaphor 65, 66
Monkey Grip 58
Moore, Brian 53
Moorhouse, Frank 79
Mora, Mirka 141
Morrison, Toni 88
Mother 5, 17
Murdoch, Iris 9, 12, 68
Murnane, Gerald 29

N

Nabokov, Vladimir 9, 12, 20, 21, 22, 68, 107, 111
Naming characters 61
Napoleon 81
Narrative voice 20
Narrator 142
Nin, Anaïs 31, 56, 77, 104
Notebooks, childhood 131
Nouns 10, 12

O

Oates, Joyce Carol 23, 29, 81
O'Brien, Edna 38
O'Day, Virginia (quotation) 46
Omniscient author 20
Overstatement 90
Overwriting 65, 67

P

Paretsky, Sarah 3
Parker, Dorothy 108
Passive voice 65, 66
Pathetic fallacy 64, 66
Philip, Alex J. 61
Pinget, Robert 22
Pitman's manual 118
Plain vanilla writing 11
Porter, Katherine Anne 14
Potter, Beatrix 95, 138, 143
Proust, Marcel 1, 2, 3
Psychoanalysis xxiii
Publishing 97

Q

Quest 113

R

Rand, Ayn 102
Raphael, Frederick xvii
Reading aloud 110, 111
Reality Notebook 51, 53
Review of Australian Fiction 133
Rewriting 13
Rhythms of prose 110
Rose, Meredith 132
Rowling, J.K. 99

S

Schulz, Charles 100
Sentences 107
Simic, Charles xxi
Snoopy 100
Spark, Muriel 5, 70, 85
Speak Memory 107
Stallone, Sylvester 102
storytelling 134
Structure of the story 142
Strunk and White 64, 90
Swift, Graham 7, 42

T

Teachers xix
Techniques 115
Third person 21
Time frame 144
Titles of stories 56
Trevor, William 107
Trollope, Anthony 86
Turgenev, Ivan 13, 27
Twain, Mark 10
Tweet xvii, 29
Tyler, Anne 17, 41

U

Understatement 90
Updike, John 22

V

Verbs 10
Vonnegut, Kurt 105

W

Wallace, David Foster 71
Warne, Frederick 95
Waugh, Evelyn 4

Weldon, Fay 9, 44, 72
Wells, H.G. 3
Welty, Eudora 18, 37, 110
West, Rebecca 13, 27
Why I write fiction 118, 131
Wilder, Laura Inglis 65
Wilson, Angus 83
Wilson, Colin 49
Wodehouse, P.G. 66, 69, 70
Wolff, Tobias 16, 41
Woolf, Virginia 23, 34, 38, 111
World of writing xvi, xvii
Writer's block 31
Writing mechanism 134
Writing to order 132

Z

Zwicky, Fay 75

Find out more about Spineless Wonders at
www.shortaustralianstories.com.au

www.ingramcontent.com/pod-product-compliance
Lightning Source LLC
Chambersburg PA
CBHW022014290426
44109CB00015B/1165